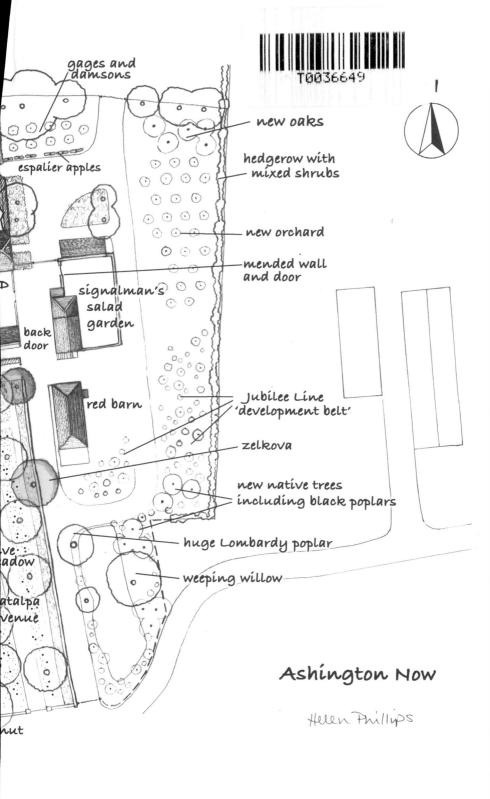

gages and damsons

new oaks

espalier apples

hedgerow with mixed shrubs

new orchard

mended wall and door

signalman's salad garden

back door

Jubilee Line 'development belt'

red barn

zelkova

new native trees including black poplars

huge Lombardy poplar

ve adow

weeping willow

atalpa venue

nut

Ashington Now

Helen Phillips

HUSBANDRY

Making Gardens with Mr B

Isabel Bannerman

PIMPERNEL
PRESS LTD
www.pimpernelpress.com

For Jo and Gail and Sarah, who made me write this book.

Pimpernel Press Limited
www.pimpernelpress.com

Husbandry
Making Gardens with Mr B
© Pimpernel Press Limited 2022
Text © Isabel Bannerman 2022
Photographs © Isabel Bannerman 2022
except for those listed otherwise on page 144

A catalogue record for this book is available
from the British Library.

Designed by Dunstan Baker
www.greygray.co.uk
Typeset in Minion Pro

ISBN 978-1-914902-94-9

Printed and bound in the UK

9 8 7 6 5 4 3 2 1

Contents

Introduction
Lord of the Flies

I am lying on the grass at the slightly higher end of things and Mr B stands defiant at the lower end of a slope. We are arguing about levels. It goes something like this.

Me: 'I am looking directly at your flies, which are open as usual.'

Him: 'That would mean the ground level here is 29 inches lower than at your end.'

Me: 'Yes, exactly, but you thought it was tit-height, which is 48 inches below.'

Him: 'I was exactly right.'

Me: 'No, you were exactly wrong' ... 'I resign' ... 'you are sacked' ... etc, etc.

This arcane banter, witnessed by architects, engineers and builders, who sometimes have to step back, out of the line of fire, can get bitter. There is something about levels, even with the aid of technology and the help of Annie Scaldwell, who is the queen of 3D in our office, which is hard to grasp and hence very fractious between us. Very sulk-inducing. But this is typical of a repetitious pattern of argument of ours, which starts with a walk round with a cup of tea on a beautiful morning and ends in bloodletting by the polytunnel. Mr B may lend grandiloquent and sage attention to my little schemes but only up to a point. Once the artillery is fired it is difficult to regroup, and generally the skirmish ends in a resignation and exhortation to 'do whatever you like'. Around elevenses the negotiations may resume amicably, and often in the ensuing days some productive other solution will somehow emerge. It is a constructive process on the whole, but it would not happen without bitter-fought wars, it seems. Design by committee never works, but then we are not a committee. We barter quite a lot; we use birthdays and Christmas to get things through. There is a sort of Whitehall element to our negotiations whereby calling it one thing means something other can be slipped through. Extending the open space on the west terrace will get through. I just need to get my timing right. My crazy-ish paving idea will happen somewhere; I just have to pick my spot, my battleground. My son will build his pizza oven but he has to understand that the United-Nations-negotiations with Mr B about this will not be rapid.

Mr B is both difficult to impress and hugely open minded. There are some people who call him a name-dropper but I always bridle and staunchly defend him. Mr B just likes to talk about anything; he likes to share and he doesn't really rate or register fame. He talks a lot and he talks to just about anything animate that will listen. He is the man to whom shop assistants and builders confide their deepest desires, because he actually bothers to ask them about their lives. He is incurably curious. He cannot, however, remember names, and calls everyone by a geographical or mnemonic tag; the builders here are called Glastonbury and Isle of Wight depending on which festival they favour. Clients are called Sheffield or Windermere depending on where they grew up. His inability to remember names, even that of his new granddaughter, and his consequent mash-up of ideas related to the person – 'Garage Doors' is one such name – is almost a syndrome. He likes people's stories; he loves to make connections, and to make people feel connected and comfortable with him. He likes to tell a story, just as his dad did or just as Rumpole of the Bailey does. This is how he drops all names, plants and people; his open mind cannot hold on to them, and he really cannot drop a plant name to impress anyone. He uses me as his 'Filofax' and if I am not there, he quite often makes names up. But he is also Mr automated-number-plate-recognition. No one but Poirot himself is a more observant witness to every detail of daily life. He startles me by saying, 'There is the daily lady's Skoda, but not in her own village.' 'How do you know it's hers?' I ask, agog. I might conceivably have known she drove a Skoda but he remembers the number plate, and spots it parked up in Rimpton and not Queen Camel where she lives. He can describe every bend in the road, every kerb mashed by tractor tyres, and the sycamore scurf that was on the puddle last time we drove this way. It is a weird kind of total recall. Getting directions from him is too much of a rural ride, but it contributes, I am sure, to his assured hand with the placing of a tree or a shrub.

His lexicon of landscape references, through experience and paintings and photographs, is huge and peopled with former girlfriends and eccentrics, stories and beauties. The pub near Stroud, where he was when Neil Armstrong stepped on to the moon, or the fence by the side of the road where he and his first wife left two thousand pounds, their running away money, in cash in a plastic bag because she had wanted to stop and see the horses, and they had hung the bag on the fence and then absent-mindedly returned to the car and left the bag on the fence for someone else shortly to find and take away. (Well, to be fair, anyone might remember that.) When he is being a beachmaster, his platoon can sometimes get overwhelmed with detail. Plant names interest him not; only what you can do with plants, the right plants, and what grows where. Place names he can do; geography was always a strong suit. And archaeology. His experience is largely visual and sensual. He is tone deaf. But the special, three-dimensional part of his brain must have expanded commensurately. This also relates to storytelling, because he always guesses the end of a film or the twist in the plot.

We both have an ability to envision almost before we have imagined a scene, and certainly before we have expressed it in words or pencil. There are moments when we both go 'ka-ching!' slipping down the same solutionary hole at exactly the same moment. There are also our total stand-offs; our loggerheads on site are like *High Noon*. But we both share this romance with houses and places. We love to come to Ashington from different angles, to spy it from the hills or see it from down the lane, hunkered as it is, our tortoiseshell and retreat. If only, we both think simultaneously, this house had been on Patson Hill, Charlock, Poyntington Down, Heavens Door, Windmill Hill, Corton Ridge or Cadbury, home of King Arthur. But here it is humble in the lowlands.

* * *

Making a garden together, in which to live and work diurnally, through thick and thin, fair and foul, is what Mr B and me like to do best. Everything else is a sideshow. It is the fourth time we have done this. Since spring 2019 Julian and I have been making a garden here at Ashington Manor Farm, South Somerset, a garden that we think of as our last principal private escapade, but you never know.

We started gardening together at The Ivy, Chippenham, in 1982, followed by a move ten years later and with two very small boys (everybody thinks we move all the time – but we move when we have to and reluctantly) to Hanham Court, Bristol, in 1993. Historical Child and Logical Child were followed by Emotional Child five days after we moved, and all three slept together for years in their dormitory in what they grew to believe was their own private Hogwarts. The move to Trematon Castle, Cornwall, in 2012 – by way of The Mount near Holt in Norfolk – was a wayward moment in which the parents were behaving badly, getting all fired up, thanks to 'Rightmove', with the idea of another whirlwind romance with a house and a garden. The Norfolk house was Bloomsbury heaven: generous but modest, with three-foot-deep neutral soil, the drive carpeted with aconites under a spreading chestnut tree and some connection with T. S. Eliot. It did not work out, and sadly you would not recognise it now, it has been ironed and internationalised beyond recognition. Hard on the heels of Norfolk, bigamously in fact, came Trematon Castle, a previous flame (we viewed it in when the lease was for sale in 2003, because we used to go and stay and festival with Logical Child's godfather nearby); this was a fatal attraction, brought back to the market at exactly the wrong moment, when we were footloose and had the cash. A place that had that unattainable quality because she belonged to the Duchy of Cornwall, she proved a wildly capricious but devastatingly beautiful mistress. Once again, we made a garden, very conscious this time that it takes ten years, a whole decade, to get a rambling rose to grow up a tree. It takes summers and winters to find out how to live comfortably in and through the garden. Our first year there it rained continuously from a Tupperware sky about twenty feet high, and we lit fires and watched the Olympics in an exhausted heap all August. Almost ten years and a knee operation later, a buyer came along, and we leapt out of the frying pan into the fire here at Ashington, in the spring of 2019. Somerset is where Mr B mostly grew up, not far away in Wells. It felt like a homecoming and the summer was glorious. We all know what came along the following March; eleven months in and we found ourselves very anxious, but in an embarrassment of gratitude to be here with Historical Child and Violet, his brand-new wife, and some hastily bought poultry, and we dug fresh beds to fill with potatoes and onions.

Following the tumultuous exit from Cornwall we set up camp in a house that had been pretty much empty for almost ten years. We whitewashed as many walls as we could and chose a pretty back bedroom full of cross light which came from windows on three sides. I scribbled down notes in bed in the morning, thinking myself the chief recorder in the household. With my second foray into garden writing, *Scent Magic*, at the printers, I thought it would be interesting to capture our hopes and fears at the start of this adventure here at Ashington. At some point I amused myself by coming up with the title 'Husbandry' for a book which might track the unlikely processes by which we work and live together. The smiles and frowns, the ups and downs, as Professor Higgins sings in *My Fair Lady*. The ladies of Pimpernel Press loved the idea, but I never kept a proper diary and when I had to get down to it, under pressure, I realised it wasn't really possible to capture especially the bigness of character that is Mr B; it would require a Dickens.

2019 was a kind of shimmering spring. For us, our new house appeared as a prism of light filtered through the marcasite panes of Elizabethan windows. Outside the amenity grass of a garden was dotted with relics of a very good garden made in the 1970s by Mrs Sandeman, Ashington's twentieth-century midwife and husbandwoman, who lived and farmed here with her husband and family from 1956 until 1986. She planted the catalpa avenue down the drive, many shrubs and trees, and many trees on the farm and along the hedgerows to replace the elms that fell to Dutch elm disease. But, apart from the cider orchard, which had won my heart in the beginning, leading the eye out to the polder-flat milk-making meadows beyond, there was not much other than viciously mown grass to behold.

As soon as we knew we were almost certainly moving to Ashington, Mr B started working out what we could sell to finance buying great beehives of mature yews. He was dogged in his determination that this garden had no moorings, was drifting about in the landscape, and that these would provide just that tethering to the ground. We sold everything we could think of to buy the yews as already mature topiary. It was a bold extravagance, but it has tied the house to its place, given it an ancient solidity which nothing else would have done for at least a decade – and we might not have that long. Mr B says that these yews provide silent watchmen. These Knights of Yew. These happy few. They are, to our minds at any rate, timeless and contemporary. As is all topiary. It somehow 'peoples' the place and commands a garden from it.

The outside is not noble or distinguished. It's not an obvious canvas for a garden maker. But it does have a feel of another world, another century. Probably the twentieth century, especially when the Merlin engine of the Yeovilton Supermarine Spitfire rumbles overhead. You can smell the cider drinking that went on in this territory of the Yeoman farmer. Indeed, there was a cider pub here that had been the heart of the farm. That it could support such an establishment is a clear demonstration of the headlong decline in workers on the land from when the Sandemans arrived to now, when three guys manage a 700-head dairy herd by racing around in their pickups. When we landed, the cider barn was still in its last young-farmers-social-club guise, with the cider press as bar, and plenty of 'Exit' signs and the nastiest toilet I may ever have encountered. Yellow as chunder. However, in the 'old days' this was the real heart of the place with, we think, the house kitchen out here – kitchens being notoriously inflammatory – in what became the green living room.

The cider pub became the studio, by way of becoming a cottage, forever to be called 'Colourful Cottage' on account of the wild paint colours I chose when doing it up. Double doors were punched out into the garden, a wide path made from here to the cosy wisteria corner and, because the walls make it feel particularly warm and sunny, irises were planted, bit by bit, all the way along.

* * *

Heritage and planning for the house took two years, during which time we laid out the bones of the garden and had, and continue to have, many discussions about the elements that make any garden, that come up time and time again in our work, but which really mattered to us personally here in our own *hortus conclusus*. Starting a garden is the beginning of tortuous relationship; the thing will never be quiescent, stay immobile or be petrified at the summit of its flowering. A garden is always in the throes of becoming something else. Mr B says: 'Garden designers tend to think it's a painting they are making, but I think it's just a fleeting dream. It is evolving, beyond anyone's powers. You cannot be prescriptive with nature. I think that's a mistake.' All those many debates about what goes into a garden often seem pointless in hindsight. The thousand tiny decisions, about which we fight like hooting chimpanzees. We nurture, till, rip up and devastate, and gently rake over each other as well as the soil and the plants. This is not about the flamboyance of show gardens, open to the public and desperate for 'year-round interest' and 'maintainability'. This is not a garden to be trampled by the curious. It has featured hugely on my Instagram because it is so central to our life, and I find the responses of my followers very heartening and touching, especially when times are tough. This garden is our retreat and our attack. And it interests me at least to examine what it is we are doing, what compels us to do it, what rules do we construct for ourselves and why? Why on earth would you do this? People often come and say things like: 'How do you have the time?' We make the time. But is it a disease, I wonder? I know it's a cure. A cure for the evils of modern life. Everybody knows that. Our garden is not frightening, it is nothing near immaculate, it is not plantiferous, it takes only a few minutes to go round and there is no processional route. It's just a manor farm garden which we love. We do it because we love it, and we love to do it.

We get asked to make gardens that are romantic; this seems to be our USP and that's great. It's a good place to be. But 'romantic' is a word that can be a bit loosely sloshed about. Where it pertains to music, poetry, painting, even in landscape design as a movement, it has a particular historical context as well as a general. But what might it mean in a garden? Romantic gardens or plots of tended land that I have loved upon the instant have a common thread: a heightened intensity, suggesting mystery while being somehow familiar and having heart. They heat emotions and shake up the imagination. History may be an element, although I think the key word is 'story', and it need not be an old story. It might be a man growing artichokes under the Roman bridge at Ronda in Andalusia, or the va va voom of tuberoses and orange blossom emanating from a tiny courtyard in Seville. I think when we begin to make a garden, we begin with a story in our minds. Storytelling is the mother of invention. The story comes from the house, the place; Arthur's Camelot at Cadbury camp is just visible from Ashington, and Glastonbury Tor also. Finding a new home and a new garden can be like sleepwalking into a sleeping place. There are places we remember all our lives. Mr B dreams about the brooding places in the rain and the moody lowering of yew monoliths. Together we feel like a child and a trespasser. Places have stories, intimations of other lives, of Eleanor Rigby, brave and careful. So compelling is the investigation sometimes, we have found places for sale and done weeks of research afterwards on the owners and the history – the murders, madmen and minutiae. It is the most pleasing occupation and teaches one a lot. A lot about history and architecture and planting. All sorts. This is what we find romantic. The choosing to settle to the thing is much harder.

* * *

The Ashington story starts with the abbeys of Muchelney and Glastonbury breaking through the swirling mists of the Somerset wetlands before they were drained. Beacons of wealth, power, and a certain welcome stability. This is the early house, vestiges of which survive here. And St Vincent's Church upon the lawn, where the bell tower is just a strange rather troubadourian chicken coop, perched upon the west end and bolstered by a rather wobbly buttress added later. The bellcote being in need of repair, a closer look at the bells revealed one of them to be dateable to around 1290. This was confirmed by a campanologist group from Bridport – and it seems that the earliest extant bells all date from this time; there is only one earlier. We chose to lay the garden out on a north–south axis using the Troubadour Tower. It is the nicest thing for miles around.

The Elizabethan story of Ashington is that, in 1566, the rather terrifying-looking and aptly named Ursula St Barbe, daughter of the middle-level squire who lived here in the sixteenth century, married Queen Elizabeth's spymaster, head of secret police and persecutor of Catholics, Francis Walsingham. One of their daughters married Sir Philip Sidney, poet and courtier to Queen Bess; you cannot get much more romantic than that. This daughter Frances appears in a portrait attributed to

Robert Peake and was godmother to Madinia, the daughter of the mathematician and astrologer John Dee. The Walsinghams spent most of their time in London and at Court, keeping on the right side of things (unlike Sidney), and the in-laws' ancient property in South Somerset, it appears, was flushed with oriel windows, lattices of glass and a grand E-shaped façade.

In 1823 half the house vanished overnight in a fire. What was left was cobbled into a five-bedroom farmhouse by dint of adding an extra floor where the extravagant double-height Elizabethan hall with oriel had survived the fire, thereby slicing the window in half with a hefty elm floor supported by massive elm beams which quickly pushed the dainty stone mullions in a southerly direction. Thus, the very oddly remodelled remnant, with chimney pieces moved around and put in backwards, lost windows and abrupt façades, remained largely unchanged until the twenty-first century. A very impressive 1980s American oak fitted kitchen and a green corner bath from Geoffrey Bonzac adorned with gold taps and jacuzzi jets were still in working order when we first set eyes on the house, which a friend was renting, in 2009 and still there when we finally moved in at Easter 2019. The deeds had passed through the Church of England and the Duchy of Cornwall in the second half of the twentieth century; the house had fallen into less sympathetic hands in this century, and had been empty off and on for some time. The smell and much else was both deeply romantic and deeply disturbing. But I particularly became fixated on how it could be put back to rights. A stipulation by Historic England that the extra floor should go urgently, and the front façade be tied back, was terrifying but also right – we wanted the big room back. While it was very hard to understand how the internal spaces would be after the structural repairs (we made a big card model of the intended layout of the house – but it helped very little), I found this conundrum, this Rubik's Cube, utterly transfixing. I was cocksure, hubris always my attendant, but we had both always wanted to live in a Hamstone house.

1
Hurray for Nettles

The thing about one's own garden – for me and Mr B particularly, because we also make gardens for other people – is that we really don't want some mirrored perfection. Obviously, this is not true of all garden designers; many make it their life's work to make their own garden matchless. But this is not our way. If you like things immaculate, read no further, or maybe do read – for enlightenment. Having had the idea to make this book, I returned to several very different models for inspiration. Mirabel Osler's never-out-of-print since 1989 *A Gentle Plea for Chaos* and Elizabeth von Arnim's *Elizabeth and her German Garden* on the one hand – wild and woolly – and the designer David Hicks and garden designer Russell Page – fiercely disciplinarian – on the other. Yin and yang. Venus and Mars. Davina and Goliath. But, although this book was premised on the acrid arguments that Mr B and I get into sometimes, and the differences of our approach on occasion, Mirabel's attitude is very like ours and fundamentally the same as that of the prolific garden writer Margery Fish. The latter has become our local benchmark because she lived nearby in a Hamstone house, with similar terrain and similar cottagey, farmhouse, middle-of-the-road aspirations. But she is much more plant-centric. The others share with us two crucial precepts: that a garden should be for living in and that plants, while fabulous and central, are not quite all that it is about. Because gardens are places to be lived in, they are about the natural world, the borrowed landscape, birds, newts, all manner of toads, as well as the unnatural world of stone, wood and whatever man-made interventions.

I would aver that gardening is all about choices, and therefore terribly bigoted and subjective. There is no 'U and Non-U', no such thing as taste or having an eye. There is only 'you' and your personal whims and fantasies. What you like may appeal to others, but that does not validate it in any way. It may help if you want to make it your business. Like clothes and housewifery it is a form of self-expression. Mirabel is fearless in her hating of things. She hated edging to beds and lawn 'made with the precision of a pre-war hair-cut'. Mr B and I quite like a straight edge. But we want everything to flow over it. Like us, Mirabel hated hypericum, calling it 'joyless', and she hated heather. 'How it mutilates the garden ... with its restricted growth and depressing meanness.' She loved unplanned self-seeding and the 'coloured smells' of cottage-garden planting, and she pleaded in her book for a little, light, shambles. A lack of seriousness in being a gardener she applauded; to drift and amble and sit about in the garden was what she wanted, to remind her of 'what life was meant to be like'. She hated a hedge trimmer, the ruin of weekend silence. Mr B does not agree about lawnmowers and hedge trimmers in the village on Sunday; I shudder to think how the sound that signals that he is happy on his John Deere tractor is shattering the quiet Ashington morning. But he does favour the loose approach to gardening. His favourite story is about a trudge round a very famous and very gardened garden; the garden staff would have naturally been embarrassed if it were not perfect, and therein lies the rub: only if you garden yourself can you determine the levels of manicure. We were part of a 'committee of taste', and our friend, an antique dealer and decorator extraordinaire, upon reaching a nice forgotten corner said, 'Oh! *Hurray* for Nettles!'

* * *

I think Mr B and I, when we are gardening at home, have always been cottage gardeners. Not so interested in the overall painting but in having the plants we love around us willy-nilly. We get fads and grow too many things. And we go off things and won't grow them for several years. Or just forget. It's amazing what you forget. Something disappears from your garden and you have no recollection it was even there. There is such a plethora of stuff on offer. Writer and plantswoman Sarah Raven's great contribution to gardening was the edit. She trialled away and told you what was worth planting and why. Fantastic.

Mr B and I strive for that sweet spot, the balance between chaos and charm that is very hard to achieve. We have always had overblown desires and too little money and help to be short on disorder and backlog, though. The key principles of this kind of gardening are not so much about maintenance, because we design to keep that practical and do-able anyway with only the help that we have got, but, of course, it's as much about the ingredients. Our abiding loves are rosemary, tobacco plants, pinks, a few cushiony roses and gravel paths. I always want salads and Mr B wants rocket, but potatoes first and foremost. We both live for spring, because the gardening is still manageable if frantic and it's all about hope and regeneration. Every year we are buoyed up by the primroses, poet's narcissi and the creamy smell of *Viburnum carlesii*. Being surrounded by what one likes, regardless, is what is important. I have a folder on my computer called 'Things I like'. It's full of everything from pictures to music. A word of warning here: this is a book about what I like; it makes no pretensions to being authoritative, or knowing anything other than my and Mr B's prejudiced, subjective and empirical inferences. Variegated plants, for instance. There is no law against them, no real rhyme or reason they are inherently wrong, but we feel in good company in our dislike of them. William Robinson, whose revolutionary promotion of wild, natural gardening as opposed to the late nineteenth-century idiom of bedding out, still sounds up to the minute: 'People are so much led by the showy descriptions in catalogues, and also [and this is the good bit!] by their own love for ugly things, that we often see misuse by the waterside of variegated shrubs – a yellow elder or a purple beech – even down to the very margins ... with variegated shrubs, absolutely the worst kind of vegetation which could be chosen for such a place.' A hundred years on and John Brookes puts it more how we know it: 'The pollution of the countryside is not only a matter of nitrates, of urban sprawl and brightly lit petrol stations; a far more subtle contamination comes from tidiness.' Mirabel Osler in the same vein writes, 'Suburban gardens are heaven in the suburbs ... but at what point does the motivation to live in "unspoilt" countryside become a compulsion to turn frenetic park keeper?' We all need to pull back and recognise the loveliness of dandelions (groan from Mr B), buttercups (agrees Mr B) and celandine (ditto) instead of this perversity of rareness and foreignness, started unwittingly by the likes of Captain Cook and Joseph Banks. I once got into very hot water with an important Cornish garden owner. When they said, surveying the serried ranks of rhododendrons and azaleas and camellias in a certain valley, 'Imagine how boring this would be if it were still hazel and hawthorn?!' I said, 'Not boring to my eyes; how much lovelier it must have been before all this invasion force was brought in by your ancestors.'

Along with the pollution comes guilt of another sort. The onus of the garden. Why do we do it? 'God Knows!' says Mirabel. It is always making one feel very inadequate, it almost creates a permanent state of discontent and a great deal of failure; maybe this is why I find other gardeners so congenial. Not keeping records of what we plant is a permanent black mark. We always mean to label and record. But we are always in a hurry, rushed off our feet and strapped for time and cash. It is a very great paradox that the informal effect is quantitively more hard work than tidiness. Hence the park-keeper syndrome. Grass cutting is a chore however you manage it. Without the seasons there would be no respite. How blessed we are to have them. It is the delirium of getting back to the garden that we both crave, the walk round together, all the uppers and downers of delight and despair. Ashington is John Evelyn's 'most glorious place without a palace'.

Evelyn's motto was 'Explore everything: keep only the best.' Perfect advice for starting to make a garden. Daydreaming, visiting places round about. Noting, not just gardens, but the cobbled pavement, the local, centuries-old way of doing things, of laying blue lias stone or standing it on its side to make a stone fence. The first summer we explored and explored with a voracious lovingness, so happy to be back in Somerset. We found lardery churches all limewashed, like Sutton Bingham, where we let ourselves in with a keypad as the service had finished half an hour since, but the inside smelled of candle grease, smoke and cool lime. We battled our way through hockey players at Leweston School into the incredible chapel which now sits on the edge of the parking lot, its ancient, silvered door always ajar, quietly leaking the tick and the tock of the 1606 clock inside the porch. The pews here are round topped like two-dimensional lollypops, cobweb grey in the buttermilk casket of the nave. At Lytes Cary, just across the A303 from us, we paid homage to botanist Henry Lyte, who translated, with his own animadversions, the Flemish herbal 'Cruydeboeck' (herb book) and, calling it *A Niewe Herball or Historie of Plantes*, created a major bestseller in 1578 – about the time that Ashington was going upmarket also. My phone is stuffed with too many pictures of the Hamstone, lias and Roman tiles of that house. The chapel has a dry oaken altar rail that I consumed for ideas for the stair we would have to build from scratch at Ashington. Outside, the yew spinning tops are justifiably famous, flanking paths of particularly fine lias slabs shouldered by lias upstands either side. *Rosa* 'Lady Hillingdon' lay languid about the parlour window. We went to what the locals pronounce 'Tintnell' (Tintinhull), and Penelope Hobhouse's classic garden with a backdrop of seventeenth-century Hamstone to kill for. We went to the Priory at Stoke-sub-Hamdon – the locals call it Stoke-sub-normal – which is most like Ashington: early, un-grand, overgrown with charm, and with a tithe barn and companion barns that we can only dream of. In similar vein, the Treasurer's House in Martock has medieval wall paintings. There is one smidgeon of such at Ashington: a wild red devil-faced angel with red wings akimbo. He is no more than 3 inches/7.5 centimetres high, his wingspan 6 inches/15 centimetres, but my god he is frightening with his ruddy face and goggle eyes, a maniacal Eric Morecombe.

In Martock town – and what a real working proper town it is – lies one of our favourite gardens, a long acre behind a street-façaded farmhouse, one of many such secret survivals of old Somerset. Fergus and Louise Dowding have been making their garden here for 26 years and it has all the passion and expression of the real deal; Louise is an extremely talented garden designer. They like to chop and topiarise their box and yew, but for all this control they both have such a soufflé light hand with the planting. Umbellifers and grasses dance throughout. A hot bit by the house is tropical with colossus plants whose leaves, by autumn, threaten to leap the garden wall and devour Martock. The street side is cool green, self-effacing but with strong box and yew against the darkly caramelised Hamstone they use there. Fergus is obsessed with a certain kind of cushioned gable, such as we have at Ashington on the oriel window. He has one similar on his house and has made a study of the masons and the dates of any such example for twenty miles or more around. Fergus is an authority on local architecture and knows all about the six churches in the area which have bell towers similar to that on the church at Ashington. We instantly made friends. Louise is a compulsive gardener but of the Osler school; she likes also to lie about watching box sets on the sofa, while the garden runs away at just the right pace beyond, *Ligustrum lucidum* amid the pigs and poppies in old untouched tin barns in the farmyard behind. Here are vegetables, a completely practical aluminium greenhouse, poppies and self-seeders everywhere, wood piles, swallows and barn owls, and a many-acred orchard falls away south, studded with brown cows. Fergus's love of all things cidery is not uncommon among cider men I have met round about and at his table. It is all consuming: the trees; the fruit; the juice; the vinegar; the apple mash 'cheeses' wrapped in hessian in the process of extraction with a press; and the fermentation, which requires much time in the cider cave, testing and footling.

Not ten minutes from Martock, due west across the Parrett River, lies East Lambrook Manor. We knew we had to return to Margery Fish's legendary garden. The eight books she wrote between 1956 and her death in 1969 were formative to our parents' generation of gardeners. She was the queen of the middle-sized cottage garden – 'as modest and unpretentious as the house'. Margery comes across as the epitome of modest and unpretentious. Her 'look' is very familiar and currently very unfashionable; crazy paving with alpine planting (very hard labour, achieved by spending a lot of time on your knees); silver and variegated shrubs along with signature 'blue' conifers; loose herbaceous perennials but nothing like a prairie, more hardy geraniums and penstemons, subtle and difficult to continue to carry off with the same flourish as the originator. What persists particularly well at East Lambrook, an absolute joy in later winter, are the naturalised bulbs. Sometimes she failed. There is a heartfelt passage about *Gladiolus tristis*: 'She has never seeded herself about for me, and many years has not even flowered. I knew a garden where they grew in dozens ... and the scent of those creamy white flowers on an evening was intoxicating.' Exactly the same failure afflicts mine, and now I think someone has dug them up by mistake and thrown them away. The garden, and hence her writing, was about manageable ambitions because Margery gardened her own garden, and for that reason her advice is always reasonable, practical, and still valid to those of us gardening away today. Our return was infused with some considerable nostalgia as we had first visited when we were first together, Mr B and I, in 1983, not so very long after Margery Fish died, her nephew still the incumbent. It was completely charming; the through way to the garden in the high malthouse might still have captured her silhouette, as Valerie Finnis had done in a rightly famous photograph.

The same adventure, with our friend, garden guru and mentor David Vicary, took us on to Melbury, Mapperton and best of all

Forde Abbey. Forde was on the list of formal canal gardens and further appealed as a house carved out of a former Cistercian monastery, in the same way our house at Hanham Court was. I vividly remember the entry through a small door into the walled kitchen garden behind the house to find, in the moment of revelation, a combination of *The Secret Garden*, *Gormenghast* and *Northanger Abbey*. The north-facing back of Forde Abbey is medieval, almost fortified, with towering walls and forbidding small windows out of which you could throw your night soil directly on to the abundant rows of vegetables below. The south front, on the other hand, is a glorious concoction of filigree Gothic trefoils, marcasite leaded lights and crazy eighteenth-century octagonal 'Gothick' sash windows puncturing a façade seemingly made of richly baked digestive biscuits. All the paint is dry and flaky – just how we like it – and the crowning glory is the long, high-lit orangery created from the former cloister, filled with clivias and sparmannia in pots, green and gold. We used it as inspiration for a 'ruined abbey' garden we created from scratch at Euridge Manor in Wiltshire. Returning to Forde just after we moved to Ashington, the magic was somehow still intact, the house blissfully unchanged, the garden better by notches owing to the arrival of Joshua Sparkes. Visual treats include blizzards of snowdrops, drifts of crocus, narcissi under magnolias, glasshouses prinked with peach blossom, dahlias scrambled with pumpkins and courgettes. It is a garden that is loved and lived, with raggedy edges, heaps of charm, not overly managed or exploited, but open to all comers. Closer to home we dwelled on the utterly biblical charm of Hinton Farm, the Red Barn farm shop to which we can walk to shop, as we did during the spring and summer of 2020. At Hinton Farm and Parsonage Farm at Mudford the Hamstone almost plays second fiddle to the rubicund Bridgewater bricks, made from Parrett clay and brough up the Parrett on boats from the seventeenth century onwards. What lesson did we draw from all this garden visiting? The English landscape is small in scale and its gardens respond to this.

* * *

Margery Fish's first book, *We Made a Garden*, was originally going to be called *Gardening with Walter*, only the publisher summarised it as 'Too little gardening, and too much Walter!' When my brother-in-law read my *Scent Magic* he said, 'Oh it's very *Gardening with Walter*.' And so the idea of *Husbandry* was born: a book about gardening with Mr B. It has proved much more difficult than I expected, and the sons and their partners comment that it is too much gardening, not enough Mr B. But here it is, and I cannot change it. Margery concentrated on her garden, and so should I. She wrote that East Lambrook was 'very spooky, you had to creep under the cobwebs' when they crawled in to take a look. This was in 1937; the house was rejected, but sometime later they returned and realised it was much better than they had first thought, rather as we did, and together they moved in in great discomfort and gradually made it warm and welcoming. She loved cottage gardens, saying that they were 'always gay and never garish', tidy without being prim (I like that) and packed with flowers. Walter was keen on tidy and liked 'a garden that is always presentable' – not one of my aspirations. He quite rightly dictated that 'a garden must not rely on flowers – but bone structure'. Mr B and I would agree, along with many others. Walter and Margery realised that 'you can't make a garden in a hurry – the only way is to live in it', and she waited 'while our ideas smouldered and simmered'. Walter's dream garden would have perfect lawns, paths, hedges and walls. Wide paths for 'spaciousness and simplicity' and paving or gravel. Walter and Mr B like lawns properly edged. They were not hitched to the Mirabel wagon. But Margery's great point is that 'I never come home without a feeling of welcome.'

The importance of homecoming, and hanging around in slight boredom, is very important to us as a family. My childhood was unexciting, but we were never really bored, and I wanted to make sure this was how the young Bs developed. We tried not to make them garden in any way that might locate it in their brains as a chore. Mr B and I find to our delight that now we are teaching the young Bs how to do their own, and, in the case of Emotional Child, other people's gardens. Historical Child is like my father in so many ways, and in gardening he is definitely a pot man, who likes to tinker around with his collection of pelargoniums. When he and Violet joined us at the beginning of March 2020, he insisted on bringing his pelargoniums. They were good ones too; they moved in and settled on every window sill. The white-fly battle was his therapy. Logical Child is the strongest, with the physique of his father but not the love of manual labour. He has the same obsessive-compulsive tendencies, his brain is always flying, and his feet need to walk when he thinks, round and round, up and down, but he hasn't found solace in turning the sod. But I think he might; he made a terrific lupin garden where he lived when at university. What he has done is lead us through the maze of renewable options for both garden and house, designing the solar garden and much that is invisible but will make it viable. Emotional Child has found solace in the earth. He loves to get a team together and make something, be it a movie or a painted cupboard, but he really relishes the contrast and release he gets from his highs of doing what he calls a little bit of 'plough'. The reward that lies in experiencing peasant, physical exhaustion, which allows for no superfluous thought beyond eating and sleeping. I think he is lucky to have been able to find this route in his urban life, and to have utilised it. Of course, Mr B loves a mission impossible – never happier than when trying to get a 12-foot-/3.5-metre-diameter root-balled mulberry tree into the Chelsea show ground. He can be incredibly know-all-y, annoying, downright rude even, but his record for getting out of holes is unrivalled and induces a fanatical loyalty. While branded with being 'extravagant' and 'impetuous', dubbed 'Lord Lavish' by old friends, Mr B is actually very careful to dream things that are doable. He knows what can and cannot be achieved while being undaunted. The *Fitzcarraldo* side of him was very much what attracted me in 1982 (Werner Herzog's film came out the year we met). We have lost our way many times and many are the times we have thought, 'What the hell are we doing here?' But I can't say it has been boring.

When making a garden take your cues from the place, the old ways, keep your requirements straightforward. What it seems is most difficult is not to iron out the charm, especially if – as with us – you have a *tabula rasa* or – equally the situation here – you have so much to sort out, such as infrastructure, drains, services and things. You know those houses that end up feeling like all the character has been flattened out of them? It happens to gardens too, if not more so. We recently had to put our foot down while working on a project where they wanted to put door closers on the garden doors in walls and gates – like fire doors at school.

De-suburbanisation was necessary at Ashington, and just a drift back to an idealised farmer's cottage garden, from the 1950s. Or so I thought. It hasn't turned out like that, of course. Perhaps because we are not farmers from the 1950s. But the gardens we have made at home are fundamentally cottage gardens. Things we like, planted as best we can. What we are really after is Welsh poppies cramming a corner with brilliant cadmium yellow, seeding themselves like a maharaja in a harem. Cottage gardens have naturally evolving planting, herbs, fruit trees, cabbages and roses jostling with hollyhocks, honesty, campanulas and pinks. This loose weave, the nearly runaway garden is much harder to achieve than a contrived garden. According to Mirabel Osler, 'It requires intuition, a genius for letting things have their head, common sense and unselfconsciousness.' Intuition is something Mr B has in shovels and spades. It is probably his greatest quality. I have noticed it in abundance in some very successful people: a genius for letting the right things go; common sense, but valuable if you can do it. Mr B has tried to teach me again and again not to over-analyse, and not to greedily read too many magazines and catch a green-eyed frenzy of covetousness. Mirabel agrees: 'But we read too many books; we make too many notes …' Oh, how Mr B agrees with this. He is always laughing at my devouring of magazines and tearing out of pages. He is right.

Nevertheless, we are both equally ill-disciplined, falling for courtesan plants laid out in the front of Waitrose and Lidl. Like fast food, these fast plants are evil in their production and unsustainable. Lord, though, it is hard to be strong when there is so much temptation out there. You con yourself into believing it is just to get you going. But it makes you feel anxious. I think we are all under the ridiculous weight of crazy lifestyle 'how-to-spend-it' pressure. And I feel stupid for falling for it, maybe even promoting it in some way. Just by setting out as a 'designer' you are part of the promulgation of this absurd myth about happiness coming from having stuff or 'lifestyle'. Increasingly, I feel bad about this, something that never entered our heads when we set out dreamily in the 1980s. But I am a huge believer in the importance of reverie. All we ever wanted to do was to play with gardens and perhaps more seriously to stem the destruction going on all about us, in some tiny way. Too tiny, I fear. Sustainability and respect for ecology is a much better tenet upon which to base one's practice, and a much stronger argument than mere aesthetics. The results of regenerative and less industrial forms of husbandry are surely more pleasing to the eye or the soul than the parking lot or the wastes of East Anglian cereal cropping. In the garden the fundamental thing is that you are making a place where you feel safe and at home. What it looks like will depend on what you like. We all long for it to look like a Sarah Raven catalogue, but the reality is, it will be a miracle if anything grows at all. If it also gives you pleasure, extends your sensual experiences with prickles and velvets, smells and rustlings, living things, edible things and colour, colour, colour, then it's definitely better than watching telly.

* * *

You need to be strong, though, and determined. Gardening and garden design is not for namby-pambies. Sometimes I can see in people's eyes, when I say I am a garden designer, a sort of sentimental vision of a dainty lady wafting around spouting Latin names and scattering seeds like Miss Wilmott. And there have been interns and people who have worked for us who, after a few weeks, request to be included in the 'artistic' side. 'Artistic' be damned. There is barely a scrag end of art involved in this garden game. It is just graft 99 per cent of the time. When you do it for other people it is about giving a service: getting the right bits together; getting people to think and work for you; letting people think it was all their idea; and making everyone enjoy the mission – in the cause of getting it all done. I once asked a builder who was digging a hole by the side of the tennis court in which a rose was to be planted if he would like to live in that hole. It was mean and small and shallow – the size of maybe a concrete block. I said: imagine you are a plant, and you must spend the rest of your life based in that hole. Would you thrive? He looked quite taken aback and some hours later I returned to find a whole series of nice loosened up planting plots worthy of *Gardener's World* and their magically very dug soil. You need a level of confidence, and this, along with marriage guidance, is what we can provide. Mr B's confidence is most admirable, and can be damned annoying. But he can instantly determine the key points and crucial notes in a place. I can do it to a certain extent. I can feel where it would be good to sit, for instance. The paths, drives and parking are always key elements. If you can solve these, you can usually transform a place.

Mr B's confidence is very important in every garden we make. I accept that he's not always right, and at home who is right is much more of a battle than at work. But at work particularly his conviction is, in itself, convincing. We are engaged to be certain and decisive in other people's gardens but at home who is the client? Our favourite motto from the choreographer Frederick Ashton, who was also a very good gardener, can lead to bitter domestic divide. He said: 'If you like red salvias, then have red salvias.' And he meant the 'bedding' sort, not the wild and sexy sort recently discovered by Jamie Compton. In the end the point about making a garden is to enjoy it. Enjoy making it, enjoy using it, enjoy it changing – as it surely will – enjoy it like a grandchild whom you can indulge and nurture.

It remains, incrementally, a struggle. We both get larger and more lethargic every winter. Mr B is amazing in how much he goes on battling away in frost and blizzard. Occasionally you might get him to watch an action movie on Sunday afternoon – but he will have done the washing up. He is a great house-husband with his compulsive ways. A curious mixture of fag-ash and furious polishing. In the garden he's not dissimilar, but unlike his father, who thought of gardening almost entirely in terms of hacking things back, he is not a true Walter. Mr B is much more nurturing. I think he really loves his plants; he gets really upset when their leaves curl or yellow and will pick the brown leaves off his pelargoniums, as now Historical Child also does. Mr B likes to feed and water plants and friends and family, on his plot, on his terms. He likes order. It took me a long time to realise what a general he is, campaigning, with military precision and detail. This fastidiousness was not altogether apparent in his appearance or habits. But his clothes and person are always clean if crumpled. I like order too. A garden requires orderliness and dedication. It really is pretty pointless thinking you can have a low-maintenance garden. It's a bad place to start. Gardening is a battle. I think Mr B is very good at solutions because he is dyslexic; getting round problems is a skill he learnt early at school. His orderliness is not conventional. Sometime his pre-planning is insane, but it is particularly necessary when gardening. Your enemies are various and generally superior. You must therefore lay the ground carefully and in advance. He hates having to do something twice.

A plan on the back of a cornflakes packet, or maybe something to scale which is measurable, is a great help for some things. To plot entrances, gateways, how and where to park, how to delineate structure, how to get round the garden in your slippers of a morning. Where are the doors to the house, portal plants? You have to think about aspect (which is why I love my phone compass to bits). Arrival is key. Cover and shelter also. Mystery and surprise. Breathers: maybe don't make every bit of your garden all-singing all-dancing – hurray for nettles – unless it's a small plot and you just love doing it. But in a normal garden the whole point of a lawn, about which I am a bit anti but Mr B thinks key, is that it is indeed a breather. It is green. Green in black and white photography is the best colour to take a light reading from. It may have to do with our vision, and the way we have adapted to seeing things, but the way light bounces back from green is very steady and readable. And I think this is why a lawn is very satisfying. So too a green hedge or a green pond. Then in contrast Mr B would say we need some showstoppers and 'events' ... be they plant based or architectural and structural. Sound and vision. Fountains and gurgling troughs. Mr B likes dead ends a lot – especially if they trick you into thinking: 'so that's all there is?' We all like a tease, the unexpected, turn a corner and be taken aback by some new dimension, topography or happening. Diversions, to stop you getting bored, but not too arbitrary or contrary; gardens can be as annoying as their owners.

* * *

If I try to think of lessons we can draw or pass on to others making gardens for the first time, I would suggest that the number one asset or approach is to observe. To really look first. Looking is a curious thing which, like watering, appears simple but turns out to require experience and training. It is perhaps at the core of what they used to teach in art school. The process of detailed observation without which everything is trite. Observation is what makes a novel, a photograph, a painting, work in the particular and be enlightening. So too with gardens or rooms. You need to really work out what you have got there; what there is to play with; why it is how it is – on account of aspect or given features; and where you can take it. Mr B's next best attribute is boldness. Whether it's planting a pot or a plot, he is prepared to make mistakes and works with confidence and gusto. Now, as a person who set out in life very timidly and who is not really apt at making pronouncements, I get that this doesn't come naturally to many of us. We don't have sufficient reserves of confidence even if we have the conviction. I think most people have the conviction, and the energy, to make their homes how they want them, but gardens are a bit trickier because they behave in unpredictable ways and change of their own volition. You need to get to grips with more levels, temporal, climatic, biological, in a garden – but it is also more forgiving. With boldness goes simplicity. Trees and grass. Gravel and sea holly. A simple idea with limited elements is almost always going to have more 'oomph' than a bit of this, that and the other. But in the end, it is all about pleasure, whether it's a little of what you fancy or a lot. Mr B tends to think more is more. He could not be described as anything but a maximalist. Sometimes this grieves me.

We cross swords over his tendency to tidy things (simply marvellous inside the house); sometimes I feel he is imposing too much – but nature is very forgiving and very powerful. All the great imposers get knocked back with a bit of healthy neglect. And he gets that. He likes to get the thing right, as Emotional Child was telling me the other day; he tackles all the rumples and creases first and *then* lets a thing go. After all this time I know he is not a Walter kind of gardener, and I understand that the quietly-running-away-with-you look – a look that Robin Lane Fox describes as the intimation that the owner died six weeks ago – requires an initial taking in hand, which we all find painful and even upsetting. Even Mr B. He said only yesterday that he never wanted to run a reclamation yard, let alone live in one, and how had he ended up like this? Now, Mr B is not a man who is afraid of mess. You can't be if you must do all these things yourself. All our life has been lived with a bag of cement in the corner of the hall, as we had to explain to a photographer from *Vogue* magazine. It's omelettes and eggs. But even Mr B loses heart sometimes. This is one reason why it is useful to do these absurdly taxing things with a companion: taking it in turns to be Pollyanna. I reassure him that it won't be like this forever.

What really motivates Mr B is the creation of a happy place. Ashington had a tangible sadness for many reasons, but I would argue it has gone. I think that maybe that is the greatest of his talents and is deeply reflected in his gardens. Mr B is very good at making pretty much anybody feel welcome and important, and so do his gardens. I would like to propose that all gardens should make you feel safe and settled, aiming for that sense of peace you get from small back gardens from Iona to Stockport. The garden as republic. This one is Mr B's and my republic, but everyone is welcome. It is intended for pleasure and for living in. Some gardens are an expression of something else, not of hospitable kindness and generosity as Mr B and I feel they should be.

St Vincent's Church and its thirteenth-century bellcote (after removal of the leylandiis), 2019.

Above: Ashington from the orchard: Mr B rakes for victory, April 2020.

Right: from Benton End: wisteria, newly planted irises, matthiola, yew beehives, spring 2020.

View from the cider house/studio,
autumn 2019.

The lawn extended west through
what was the lockdown vegetable
patch, spring 2021.

Looking south: the lockdown
vegetable garden, 2020.

Overleaf: Urns and ferns, the nut
tree garden, 2022.

They may also be about wonder and surprise, but they must primarily be about warmth and the ability to be open and relaxed in them. I do think it is interesting as a principle. Mr B draws great pleasure from whatever he does. We are both hedonists; our preoccupation with scent and colour is about hedonistic responses. We pour in love and affection, and that is what we want others to get out of it. Pleasure.

Perhaps he does this by first eliminating the negative. If there's a problem identify it, face up to it. Deal with the key issues: boundaries, ugliness, awkward layout, soil and aspect. What is your goal? I would put first a sense of enclosure and safety. Ownership and fun possibilities. If you can, you want to inhabit it either as a backdrop from inside if you are very short on space or, if you can get a table and drag a chair out, as a bower of smell and flower – at least for a moment. It may only have a small moment. You may only manage to grow some mint in a pot for your potatoes and cocktails. But hang on to your daydream. Daydreaming is a skill that should be on the school timetable. It was in fact the point of school; it taught one to get through the boring tasks which must be done through the distraction of private fantasy and visualisation. This is exactly what gardening is for me. A garden is but a fleeting dream. You cannot trap or hang on to it. You can only hope to grasp at cobwebs of wonder: the irises this year; the martagon lilies next year.

* * *

There was a garden we found in Ronda in Spain on our first holiday together, in spring 1988. We took cheap flights to Malaga and hired a Fiat Panda for a week for £50 and drove round Andalusia, which was still recognisable from *Two Middle Aged Ladies in Andalusia* (1961) by Penelope Chetwode; by which I mean, still recognisably medieval. Widows in black poking at donkeys; little piles of burning rubbish, which you also found in India. It was enchanting. In Ronda we looked down at the 400-foot/120-metre El Tajo gorge from the elongated eighteenth-century bridge, at the circling raptors as the vaporous wafts of town sewage floated up from the river below. Every evening we kept watching two brothers tending their small patch perched on the cliff about halfway down. We could see artichokes among olive jars and trees clinging to a whitewashed house. Little beds of leafy greens ringed about with limey paths, and mammoth catering tins printed with colourful pictures of tomatoes and peppers used as containers. Eventually we found a way down the side of the precipice below the houses that are now expensive hotels and restaurants but then were mostly empty, strung out along the cliff's edge. We got all the way to their garden, teetering vertiginously with the great river below and the great bridge above. We found them asleep among their plants, it being the afternoon, but having been woken up by such unlikely intruders they showed us every last tomato and blade of coriander in their precipitous Eden. It was bounded on one side by cliffs and steep scrub and on the other by the staggering cliffs over which the bodies were flung during the civil war fifty years before. For company there were Bonelli's eagles with a wingspan of six feet. This patch was the brothers' kingdom and their larder. It was very heartening. Where they got water, I cannot imagine.

2
Ashington Manor Farm

lear as a bell the early morning light filtered into a room where the stone transom was oddly the same level as the floorboards and the window to the right was clearly only a quarter of a window, a series of Gothic stone cusps or ogee lintels but right down by the floor. I was fully clothed and in bed and stiff with cold. It was January 2012, and we were at Ashington, having stayed overnight with Yseult, our dear friend who was living here. Yseult is an architect and writer, and fate had brought her and her husband, Mark, to Ashington as tenants. In return for the loan of the by then barely functioning house, Yseult was drawing up all the applications to move Manor Farm and its buildings to a virgin site elsewhere on the seven hundred acres and restore the Manor House, the attendant farmworkers' cottages and farm buildings, some of which had already been sold off or rather successfully converted. Mark and Yseult and their grown-up children loved the house at Ashington passionately, but by 2012 Yseult was a widow dealing with Mark's death and the Inland Revenue. We had just moved to Cornwall, but we tried to swing off the A303 and see her whenever we could. She held herself together with stoic fortitude, but the house had become a theatre of grief; she had a bad accident with the horrible old cooker, and her son was haunted by violent ghosts, nothing worked, the taps dribbled blood rust and she existed, sleeping often with Rollo her spaniel in the kitchen by the wood burner, too cold and miserable to go upstairs. So much emotion ricocheted through the house but she and I would pour over and over the plans with a manic intensity.

This particular faraway morning was a gleaming one, frost bright. I went downstairs and outside and filled my lungs with air like crystals. The gravel was hard with rime, crunching a beat to the jackdaws squabblings on the barn roofs facing a faintly warm sunrise. You cannot save people, but it sometimes feels like you can save a house. Mr B was genuinely surprised when I came in for breakfast and suggested it. Yseult has always been completely behind it, providing expertise and inside knowledge. But it was not remotely possible for us then, and would not be for another seven years. We were in the throes of trying to make a garden at Trematon and make living in Cornwall work. We could not and should not even think of such disloyalty. Yseult thankfully moved to a home of her own and Ashington remained stubbornly empty, overpriced and unloved. Nobody could get their heads round the geometry of the structural stipulations. The authorities wanted the house taken apart before the front wall fell off and then put back to something more like it was before the fire of 1823.

Ripple dissolve more than half a decade and a miracle happened at Trematon and we were offered enough money to escape the burdens of the Duchy lease. It took nine months to tie up, during which time we scoured the country for anything with a bit of magic that was affordable. We found one house in that time which would have been better, in that it had been done up beautifully already and what it needed was our thing: a garden. Finding the cash is always the problem, and always means going for the restoration option as this can be done slowly as dribs and drabs of money can be eked out. We were engaged to another house at Stalbridge, but there was a legal hiccough which made it impossible to buy immediately. In January 2019, in the late afternoon, I suggested to Mr B that we take the turning for Mudford just to see the sunset at Ashington. How warm the walls breathed on the west, the Hamstone riddled with holes where the masonry bees were hibernating. The flat lands stretched north towards the Levels and Wells, where Mr B had grown up. The light on the television mast on the Mendip horizon was just visible in the gloaming. Curiously, this same mast was always just visible on the southern horizon from Hanham Court, and it always made me think of Hilda, Mr B's marvellous mum, and feel comforted. I feel the same now. After a harum scarum exit from Cornwall, which involved three weeks on an air bed waiting for the money *after* the completion day, it was Maundy Thursday 2019 when we rocked up the catalpa drive in two motors stuffed to the gunnels and, having blown up the air bed again, hardly slept with the excitement.

* * *

The catalpas down the drive. So odd a choice of tree. Being 'down the drive' they are the first thing anybody notices after the little church of St Vincent to the west of the entrance; this is a tiny chapel really, tethered on the lawn and mucked around with by the Victorians, although not entirely divested of its early charm. From the late 1950s a lovely farming family took on the tenancy of the farm and house from the Church Commissioners. Mrs Sandeman was reportedly and evidently interested in plants and gardens. She gardened here and I often think about her. She chose the catalpas to go two by two down the drive. On a high summer's evening they add an equatorial feeling to the place, a touch of Karen Blixen. The Sandemans were from Rhodesia, I think, so maybe it was some subconscious yearning to be back there that led her to plant them. But my tutorial criticism would be that they create a Narnia effect, always winter but never Christmas, for much of the year. There were two huge catalpas in the square in London where my parents lived, which was otherwise entirely barren paving. They were the only green thing and so there was nothing to compare them with, and they came out about the same time as my father's basement fig, in early June; they were magnificent. In Somerset the whole landscape has been aflame with hawthorn and elder before their leaves so much as sniff the air, their branches doggedly grey and naked. However, on a plot with virtually no trees, they are Ashington's crowning glory.

At the top of the drive, hard by the magnificent bay window paid for by Walsingham's spymastery, stands an Irish yew, aristocrat of the evergreens, high as the house, whose age is uncertain. It is annoying for casting such shade upon the now newly revealed expanse of window, but I love it for the birds that dive-bomb the garden from this moving tower. Any breath of wind excites a clattering of its mahogany branches like chopsticks. It is attended by several pages in the form of lanky box trees, of some age also, which Emotional Child and Mr B clipped and sculpted in 2020. They will turn into 'Niwaki' clouds. The purpose, though, was to let light into Mr B's bulb oasis beneath, where originally some *Cyclamen hederifolium* lingered with three clumps of some rare, fat and grey-leaved snowdrops. Perhaps they were planted by Mrs Sandeman for there is also periwinkle, a last resort plant for anyone running out of time, an old rugosa rose and – pleasure of my heart – several wild eglantine roses.

Parking and cars. Here we are in minefield territory. Mr B and I have yet to resolve the parking 'issues' which, on a job, would be sorted at the beginning, but at home we tiptoe round this one for the moment. As the gravel right in front of the house, which I think adds to the shoddy prep-school malaise that lingers here, is currently the builder's yard and elevenses patio, all arguments are on hold. We are currently using, instead of the drive, the concrete road to the farm between a low wall and the pond on the east. This is how I would like things to stay; everyone would park their cars round the back if I had my way. In the front ... but Ashington is one of those houses, especially now that we have put the room arrangement back to *ante ignem* – before the fire – that cannot really decide where the front door is, the porch having burnt down or been taken down after the fire and the cross passage blocked up on the front. This is probably the single saddest thing for Mr B; he really does dream and talk regularly of putting back the porch and opening up the fabulous Hamstone doorway into the kitchen. In making our new but old-style 'Gormenghast' kitchen we have had to block up the second cross passage door in order to have any walls upon which to put furniture in the room. In the old pictures of the farm there was a carriage turning circle of grass in front of the 'new' porch. The new porch is a travesty, on this Mr B and I agree. It seems to have been 'reclaimed' and 'repurposed' from somewhere else, possibly the church hard by, but by rogue traders who did not understand how to put the arch back. It looks more like the work of hobbits than of Somerset stonemasons. We are agreed that with the builders gone, the planting round it to 'lose' it totally will begin. It will be lost. As to the carriages: I don't think you can change the natural flow of things, and there is a logic in driving to the front door so I am not yet convinced that my idea – which is to make a Margery-Fish-style garden here, all crazy paving in the south-facing heat – will work. I can hear Mr B's stomach churning at the mention of the 'crazy' word. But we do have a lot of bits of broken lias slab, and it can look very pretty with plants growing all through it. I think it might have a retro chic. The drive is not long and not imposing. We have tried to give it that 'lost domain' feeling by letting the grass grow in the middle of the track and letting the grass grow long to the sides. Mr B moved his considerable snowdrop collection in here; they are friends from friends – Christopher Gibbs, Alice Boyd and Mary Keen – plus a huge number he blagged from the lovely lady whose house we could not buy, where they grew under the biggest horse chestnut in Dorset. Mr B says keeping the builders from trampling them was his greatest labour of love.

The letting go of the drive grass was never for one second under discussion; it just happened. With the end of a ten-year boot camp of mowing the life out of everywhere round the garden, including the orchard, the buttercups sprang up to greet us, and the early purple orchids, and we added everything but the kitchen sink, so thirsty were we for vital signs of life: fritillaries, snowdrops, aconites, *Tulipa sylvestris*, camassias and Himalayan cow parsley. Maybe it's all too much. But this side of the house has a propensity to look like an institution, and it now looks fantastic in spring, a *primavera prato* of delights. We have just had to be patient as the front has been covered with scaffolding for a whole year. Mr B is much more patient than me. It has potential, it is Hamstone and hot, and it has all the trees on the plot. It has the great upturned besom of a Lombardy poplar by the pond, dominating it and the landscape for flat miles. Right by the house on the east side is another evergreen. Not such an aristocrat, *Calocedrus decurrens*, the incense cedar, must have been planted in the 1970s right near the old kitchen. Because it is a cedary smelly cypress which looks like a thuja, and is one of the biggest trees on the property, I have chained myself to its preservation. Mr B is right, of course; it will have to go. It also lets nothing grow beneath it. It is not just ungenerous, but it has killed many rare precious snowdrops and all the cyclamen, aconites, honesty and honeysuckle we have tried to succour in its shadows. It is a sociopath, creating a dry acid world in its pall. But it's a bargaining chip. It would fit my front drive transformation plans to remove it. We shall see.

Nearby is a zelkova, another interesting choice, rare-ish, endangered; people thought it might be a good substitute for elm at the time of their annihilation. Both Mr B and I salute Mrs Sandeman for insisting on replanting proper indigenous trees all along the lanes when the elms came down. She planted limes and maples which are respectable, but nothing, even in a hundred years' time, will make up for the elms in this and so many other landscapes. When we came to dissect the guts of the house here, we found that every last door jamb and stud partition was made of elm. Elm trees must have littered the lanes, leaping up like rushes in ditches, staggeringly tall, long-lived and broccoli-headed. Elms gave a scale of verticality to the landscape which is completely inimitable. Zelkova will not do it, nor the black poplars which are my favourite replacement, a noble tree which we have planted here by the dozen.

We have to forgive the house its truncated appearance, and all that whiff of the institution that the south side has as you approach, for it is only half its former self. This is part of its allure as well: a grand thing cut down. Inside, it has the proportions of a big house but a limited number of rooms. My friend Fergus tells me that the opulent bay window on the south, the Walsingham window in our shorthand, is of a type which came almost as kits from the masons of Ham Hill in the later sixteenth century. The façade, before the window, was almost certainly flat or had another 'nose' gable on the west end making it the classic E shape we associate with Elizabethan houses. It would have come, he thinks, with its characteristic 'kneelers' either side of the gable at the eaves; they appear all around here in different shapes and sizes and this one is big, all cut and ready for your local journeyman to fit. Like an 'Everest Double Glazing' franchise and, of course, they fitted the best. But punching a hole in your existing walls and banging in the newest super-light existential glazing was risky even with master masons abounding. It feels as though the structural elements went wrong rather quickly as the side panels of the bigger downstairs embrasure were infilled within a hundred years.

The engraving at the beginning of this book, on page 7, was made in 1819, exactly two hundred years before we turned up in the story and just over two hundred years since this window was put in. But the extraordinary thing is that it captured, for *The Gentleman's Magazine*, the house in all its olde worlde glory just four years before half of it burnt down. There are no other records; no archaeologist has found the footprint because the farm buildings went up in the intervening years. Even when, upon instruction from Historic England, we took the house apart in an effort to stabilise and stop the elevation falling completely off the front, we found very little that helped to explain the original layout pre-inferno, or quite how they had castrated it. The more we unpicked it, the less clear it became. It was as though it had been rebuilt by hooligans. All that was holding it up appeared to be plaster, horse-hair and some lath which was made of straw. It felt like a rushed job. Bits of broken masonry, mullions and transoms, heads of windows were bunged into walls willy-nilly; whole fireplaces carted about and dumped in new places, in a corridor. Mr B is convinced the head of his beloved porch door was turned into the head of the sitting room fireplace and turned back to front – for if you put your head up the gargantuan chimney breast and look inside, there are four delicately carved quatrefoils, blackened and soot-laden. The most catastrophic brainwave that somebody had was to gain one extra bedroom by means of reusing elm beams to make a mezzanine floor across the great hall and its oriel window. Who needs a draughty old place like that? The insertion of a floor at this point, pushing on the window with force, necessitated the removal of the original ceiling of the great hall. Was it highly decorated with pendentives and wild men eating forbidden fruit? Up where this might have been was a bedroom with windows only your feet and knees could see out of. It is hard to explain. The ground floor meanwhile became dark under low ceilings.

Nothing changed between the 1820s refashionment and the 1950s, when the Sandemans carved out some bathrooms and persuaded the landlords, the Church of England, to reinstate the stone-tiled roof (swapped for cheap slate after the fire) – at huge expense. The poor old house, however, bearing the roof on its oak frames and fifteenth-century wind jambs, found first that all the weight was lifted, with attendant structural consequences, and then weighed down again in 1976 with solid stone. It is a very beautiful roof and the house much better looking for it, but it is fascinating that at the time nobody seemingly even peeked at the foot of the trusses to see how little contact they had with the masonry below. Ashington's secrets were just biding their time. However, we foresaw only a little of this. We knew we were in for a rough ride, but we had a dream.

* * *

Ashington, then, was a curiosity of a building, set in the bastardised remnants of a working farm with an acre of cider orchard, four acres of back field and a garden of mown grass up to all doors. The house a fragment of a once much larger Tudor house made from a medieval house, on the alluvial planes of the lazy river

Yeo, near what Thomas Hardy called 'Ivel', which makes us rightly think of dairy herds. Both nearby Mudford Sock and Chilton Cantelo boast neat late nineteenth-century red brick houses with stripes of glassy black glazed stretchers, designed reputedly by the same Thomas Hardy, architect. Perhaps he walked over to see the slightly wonky, warm-as-a-ginger-biscuit Ashington Manor, cosseted, as many farms round here are, by a bevvy of ruddy brick outbuildings. When we took over, we found not so much Margery Fish's cobwebs, but a house and garden that reeked of that dank flavour that sharpens all the senses. Aware as a dog of new smells in new territory, so different from the estuarine damp of south Cornwall we had left, the unfamiliar-smelling plants in the new garden assaulted my mind. There were, of course, familiars like lilac and hawthorn and cow parsley humming with hoverflies attracted by that smell which is just slightly dispensary. It was that brief honeymoon of possibility. The birds had never seemed more insistent, talking in the early morning in their languages of the hedgerow. Never louder, the thrum of bees among the pear blossom in the astonishing warmth of April afternoons. Never more tonic, the freshness from the balsam poplars behind the tin barns at gloaming, and that metallic smell unearthed by the bean and pea seedlings in the thankfully organic fields surrounding us after brief rain.

The new garden was in both my and Mr B's imagination to be therefore a yeoman's domain, an honourable place of husbandry, a pre-war Somerset from picture books we scoop up in Sherborne market every Saturday, barely a garden at all for me. For Mr B it was about childhood gardens, as he was brought up largely in Somerset, just north of here. The house sits tawny, almost a beached ark, upturned in the somnolent watery lushness, ditches purring with fecund frogs. Any 'gardening' needs to be sleepy and understated but practical, the washing always flapping above the vegetables. Whomsoever tended my fantasy garden loved a scented flower but struggled as I do with vegetables. Cottage gardens were always conjured with flavour-providing flowers and leaves, with herbs, with crossover culinary and perfumery plants such as pinks and marigolds, and with 'strewin' plants to make rooms and pillows smell good – hops, lavender, rosemary. Simple stuff, all the 'sweet' charmers: sweet William, sweet cicely, sweet rocket, sweet alyssum. We would plant sweet Nancy among the throngs of primroses and violets already here, and precious corners of muscari, hyacinths and lily of the valley. We would plant the *vulgaris* and the *officinalis*, the common and apothecary plants: *Paeonia officinalis*, *Rosmarinus officinalis* (now *Salvia rosmarinus*, but never mind) and *Thymus vulgaris*. The *Lavandula* formerly known as either *vulgaris* or *officinalis* is now *angustifolia* – and you can find one called 'Vera'; much of ours came from B&Q without a name. I find lavenders strangely complicated and difficult to grow. But the idea was to grow a scented poem, a prescription for happiness, that might be bunched in a jug – lavender, rosemary and fennel with perennial stocks. We want all the *foetidus* and the *odoratus* plants, the foul and the fragrant; *Iris foetidissima* – the roast beef plant – and *Helleborus foetidus* complemented by odorous *Lathyrus odoratus*, *Daphne odora*, *Ribes odoratum*. Plants grasped from the meadows, the hay scents of lady's bedstraw, bulrushes, briar roses, flag iris. This kind of planting would keep things levelled and no-nonsense; silage, first cut hay, the deepest smell in the lanes and meadows.

It is a very understated formula. It needs to avoid being precious at all costs. As I've said, I pleaded for mercy for the shaggy incense cedar, whose smell assails me near the dustbins, because, although it is not the obvious choice for the bucolic, Samuel Palmer vision we have, that is exactly why it needs to stay. Life and gardening are all about contradictions. I argued that the cypress should stay for its mountain smell and to remind one that there are other places, high in altitude, even legendary, but none smell like home. But I think I am relenting; the cedar may have to go. We are planting so much in its place and everywhere. Immediately we talked of where to put more musty plumes of lilac, *Syringa vulgaris* of muddled hues and muddled-headed scents to be followed by *Philadelphus coronarius* – the first to flourish each summer and followed by the later-flowering forms such as *P.* 'Monster' with its huge stamen-bossed blooms. The lost garden in the undergrowth suddenly burst with those all-surviving species: peonies smelling of cold cream and the aforementioned briar roses where the cars park, which put forth a pong of apples and horse piss after the rain. This is very much part of that most potent welcome that Ashington gives you. If you end up arriving at somewhere else, we will have to plant *Rosa rubiginosa* there also.

The wisteria flowered in a corner where a pregnant bit of wall plopped out and had to be rebuilt as soon as we sat there. It is the perfect place to sit, cossetted in the corner which became known – because we planted all the irises we brought with us, and then some more, there – as Benton End (after Cedric Morris's house in Suffolk). Others had got there before us, planting the pretty, late-flowering, long-raceme-bearing wisteria variety, but not highly scented. Near it a rather gaudy rose opened, heavily scented with Bulgarian attar. We needed to plant deep-cushioned smelly roses such as *Rosa* 'Étoile de Hollande' followed by rampant rambling roses, *R.* 'François Juranville' smelling of ripe apples, and in late July when the tin barns tick with the heat, the pert buds will open of creamy *R. moschata* 'Autumnalis' pushing out perfume. Come September branches will bow with a bounty of prunus, greengages, damsons and bullace. And there will be quinces perfuming the larder. For winter picking we can plant lightly almond-smelling *Prunus* × *subhirtella* 'Autumnalis' somewhere, although Mr B thinks it always a disappointment, and shocking pink *P. mume* 'Beni-Chidori' to put in a jug on the sill where the cat sleeps. Outside the kitchen window, tucked in dry against the house, we'll enjoy the forgotten tufts of Algerian iris, scented when brought indoors in February. Bowls of bulbs will be coming on in early winter: *Iris reticulata* and hyacinths among the scented pelargoniums that might make good cat's names – Clorinda, Mimosa and the tomcat Attar. I dream on. Mr B raises his eyebrows and calls me a fantasist. Mr B makes my fantasies come true.

3
Structure: Stops & Starts

Our aims were not revolutionary or grand. A country garden, designed to borrow from the world beyond its boundaries, but essentially horticulture in tandem with the needs of outdoor living. The same aim, expressing a private paradise, has been at the root of private garden-making from Pliny's garden near Ostia to Kellie Castle in Scotland. A place of tranquillity, where the idea of the house spreads out across the garden and the potting shed creeps back into the porch and beyond. We need, Mr B and I, in our work and at home, to marshal the attributes of the site and arrange them in what might be deemed priorities. The intention is always to intensify and concentrate the *genius loci*. To move the garden into the 'otherness' of an unknown place.

Levels play a great part in the composition of a garden. Changes in level should be handled, says Russell Page, 'with discretion and conviction', but as we saw at the beginning of this book, they are the subject of much sore argument in this household.

I think things get heated because levels are very difficult to get your head round, very difficult to express in words and on paper, requiring a particular kind of brain, one that is both comfortable with three dimensions and able to express itself clearly. Luckily Ashington is flat as a billiard table. Coming out from the house a breadth of ground around that is level is usually a good idea, so that the house does not appear to be tumbling away or, worse, the opposite problem, that feeling of almost stubbing the toes and nose on account of the nearness of walls or climbing terraces. Levels being less of a problem on the Somerset Levels, we have plenty of room for this all important 'plinth'. You generally need to come out on to a path, and in my ideal garden you should be able to make a dewy morning circuit in slippers or sneakers, which means dry gravel or paving. A crucial part of that sentence is the word circuit. It helps to be able to go round a garden of any size, rather than to the end and back, for a path where you have to retrace your steps is irksome. Curved shapes, somehow, we find difficult. A client once said to us during a presentation, 'I see you are both very fond of a right angle!' Yet nature abhors a straight line, which means you can start off with a plethora of sharp angles and let her do the messing up. Good bones and underlying structure with well-made paths, walls and well-defined changes in levels are what me, Mr B, Russell Page, Walter and David Hicks all like.

David Hicks so liked a straight line that he once sent back to us our bread-and-butter postcard which he had ruler-ed with red biro all over the front. The postcard was an aerial view of the formal courtyard at Wilton, a round pond within a pleached lime square – designed by our friend David Vicary – only it was not square. It was not true. A wandering path and what he called 'that hideous mess of sick' (daffodils in grass) were anathema to him. His book *Garden Design* probably taught us more about design in general than any other and I have several copies, the kindly inscribed hardback glued together after a flood. His interiors were everything I wanted to get away from in my teens. But this garden book, very simply illustrated almost entirely in black and white, was a revelation.

My biggest diversion, after reading, acting and directing, dressmaking and doing other girls' make-up in the endless boring times at boarding school, was the darkroom. Sister Daniel, a genuinely good person with real emotional intelligence, decided to start a photographic club with us when we were her form. I cannot remember now but I think we were lower four, so twelve years old. I loved it, and I think the world of black and white photography. Like line and life drawing, these things are a key visual training. Mr B was a really good black and white photographer. In his teens he made a first collection of things gleaned from junk shops, and what he sought was old camera equipment and early photographs, including calotypes and daguerreotypes. A few years later he made good money but now some of the prints and cameras would be even more hugely valuable; he lent some to a museum in Paris, but lost track of them. A very few of his own early images survive; they are abstract, using the textures of windblown sandstone on the outside of Durham Cathedral and those radiator colossuses inside. My apprentice photographs were of my friends at school, heavily made up by me, looking mournful and moody. Black and white photography is primarily about the beautiful and multifarious greyness of grey, the hinterland between black and white, the darkest grey and the lightest grey. When taking a light reading, green, especially grass, is your median, your most constant light. Green is your grey. Green is the composition medium of a garden. David Hicks's book is illustrated almost only with black and white photographs, with two batches of colour photographs of green-only gardens, such as the one Keith Steadman made at Wickwar in the 1970s. This showed that if your design works in black and white, it will work in colour. It will work. Colour in the gardens that we find pleasing is just the sprinkles: the structure and punctuation must 'admit no errors'.

Architecture and an assured underlying structure are for Mr B and me the starting point. We are not primarily, perhaps not even instinctively in my case, plantspersons. We know what we like but our approach to garden-making does not start, I think, with plants, although plants are crucial for mood, and we have centred designs around collections of plants such as irises, snowdrops, hellebores or ferns. Before plants the elements that define a garden are: paths; walls; well-defined changes in levels; pools and canals; paved sitting places; sheltered spots to picnic or nap; good edges; wooden leaf gates (maybe with a grill to see through and let the frost sink away); limestone; cobbles (never granite setts except in granite places); trellis; tables with seats at which to sit and enjoy the garden. Not, on the whole, a hard chilling stone bench for me and Mr B. The artefacts in a garden, says Russell Page, 'should be summary, direct, and apposite'. I think he means 'do not besmirch my composition with bits of tat'. Furniture in particular is difficult and expensive. At home we have 'oughts and umbles', old things, mismatched (Nancy Reagan is supposed to have said when shown Robert Kime's decoration of Andrew Lloyd Webber's duplex in New York, 'Oh my, how original. Nothing matches'). This is for reasons of economy, and also because we like that look from a world before there was a mass market in plastic garden furnishings. The architectural elements are important to us for creating an impulse to go somewhere, to be drawn to use different bits of the garden, usually at different times of day. Structures – arbours, pergolas, fruit cages, chicken houses, glasshouses, donkey sheds and tool sheds – are also invaluable as a backdrop to planting. Page is right in saying that slavish following of even the best models of garden architecture can end up looking sententious and laboured. It is very difficult to pull off a new garden building, and I know some of the things we do are not as light-handed as we might have hoped. Architecture is like making scones: some people have the lightness of hand, they can make things that are complete, discreet and yet pretty. The clue for garden buildings is perhaps for them to be proportionate in their mass and weight but be simplified to the limit as regards their detail. Structures in most gardens are foils and supports for plants, which add their own decoration. But above all, I think, you need to remember that a garden is a home for growing things.

The degree of formality one employs is going to depend on the character of the house and the idiom of the landscape. Ashington is primarily a farmhouse, but with Elizabethan pretensions on one side and an ancient range to the west which is more contemplative and monastic. This west side suggests a story more enclosed and productive to me, herbal perhaps, reflecting the medicinal purposes of the first botanic gardens such as Padua, watered down to almost homeopathic levels. It needs only a hint of some suggested purposes, understatement in everything. There is no need to build a slavish 'reproduction' medieval garden here, and what would it be but bogus? The imagination is free to build its own elaborations. Exact reproductions transposed from features admired elsewhere usually fail to achieve their intended effect. It is fundamentally important in a large garden and landscape to understand the context and history.

The factors that will suggest the theme may well be some predominating elements of the site. Here, we have level grass, an orchard, some rough hedges, the house and barns, the potting shed – this last being crucial as it is inside the garden and so, luckily, a way through from one garden to another potential garden. These not-so-incidentals help one find a point of departure. The house, the neighbourhood, the wild flowers, walls, ditches, whatever. Here we identified upon the instant that we wanted lawn and topiary à la Lytes Cary. We knew what we wanted to say, but we needed to express it as straightforwardly as possible. The directness and simplicity of this approach requires discipline and courage. Things Mr B has in spades and shovels. I have learnt slowly, I hope, from Mr B. I think we both continue to teach ourselves to pare things down; we need to cut back the tendency to egg things up. It is hard, but you recognise it in gardens that leave you satisfied, that balance and confidence which Page calls 'reticence in a garden scene; a simple idea developed just as far as it could be'. Constraints can be constructive. A garden which has to be shady is an opportunity for such calm and calculated planting: yew, holly, ivy, and maybe acid green. In the same way a garden which is very acid or very limey imposes a coherent and simplified planting. Make an advantage of a disadvantage. A garden is its own small world. Each world is different, has its own nature, yet is part of the wider world. But a mixture of mannerisms, taken from today's myriad and bombarding pictures, exhibitions, histories and designs, can lead us merely to allusion rather than style; allusions are there in our thinking all the time, but somehow, we must stop them becoming platitudes.

* * *

Start with paths. Here at Ashington you fell out of every door into a rug of tufted lawn. There are sweet photos of us with rugs and broken chairs outside the west door, on the grass with the Morrisons picnic tables we bought on Good Friday. It was that treasured moment, camping in a place when all is possibility. I have friends who have managed to capture and keep that moment; to live like we think people lived in the 1970s with a record deck by the open window. But it wasn't long before the mini digger arrived. It was the drains what did it. The drain run was beside the west-facing wall of the house. Where it went no one knew. But the contents were not going wherever they should, and that was a problem. In digging up the drains and replacing them we took out the trees that had self-seeded in front of what is now the studio but was then a corner with a broken-down lean-to privy which had a certain charm. They used to be everywhere, forgotten conveniences round the back where no one noticed, surrounded by nettles and elder, smelling of cool crumbled plaster, a chain still swinging from the high-level cistern. I was sad to see it go. We pulled out a plinth with the mini digger, making a big terrace with self-binding gravel. By doing this we were bringing the gingery warmth of stone horizontally out into the garden. Unusually, Mr B thinks it plenty big enough. It is I who have fantasies, imagining long lunches playing at pretending we live in the Luberon on this terrace. It is definitely not big enough, I keep saying, and is an example of the problems that come from not making a proper plan at the start. But at some point, maybe when we can afford to pave it, we will take out the planting along the lawn and push it out a metre further to the west. I bet it looks less interesting and I regret it.

By this act of making the terrace, we were off. One path leads inevitably to more paths, but only where necessary, going as directly as possible from place to place. Curved paths are harder to manage, Mr B and I find, especially on flat ground. If you draw a wavy line on a plan, it can look very mannered. But sometimes it happens without a moment's consideration. The lilac and honesty beds at the front of the house just became curvy island beds, which might have been suburban but they work with the trees, which dictated winding paths from the start. In the winter nut-tree garden, the format is a cross with a central circle (it is amazing how often that London Underground motif pops up in our drawings) round the nut tree, but the natural planting (and the mole) obscures any rigid geometry. A browsing line from deer or cattle is always a thing of marvel and beauty, such precision, straight line against curve, but straight lines are not common in nature, except for stone laminations and horizons, I suppose. Paths draw the structure of a garden plan and the stronger and simpler the lines the better. After a bit of scribbling and scrapping with each other, we agreed to scrape out two paths going west, thus forming a three-sided rectangle. Taking the Troubadour stair on the north and the door from my inner sanctum office – later to become the great hall – to the south, we drew parallel lines in hoggin heading west. The point of the paths here is to delineate the shadowy marks of a vestigial *hortus conclusus* – suggesting a long-lost garden in the European medieval manner, an enclosed flower garden for pleasure and leisure and flirting when all around was wild, heath and forest – metaphorically acknowledging the medieval make-up of the house.

To each side of this courtly court of a garden we planted rosemary, domesticated as a cat. We didn't know much else. We barely had a fag packet plan at this point. Running on intuition we were for the moment in parallel and agreed. A well-kept lawn would be good here, even I would admit this, set about with hedges and topiary. Big lavender, old English we had in mind, in long lines, along with pinks and columbines. Once upon a time we would have planted miles of box. One of the few fine things already here are the scattered bits of box, long grown out of hedges into trees, big enough to be bomb-proof from disease. They give off that waft which is essential to old England gardens in my smell map. A plan did emerge, but we are usually too busy to draw up our own garden. However, we did do it here, partly for planning permission, but also because it becomes essential with a formal layout to plot paths and gates; how and where to park (still contentious); doors out from the house; and to fix in one's brain the compass points and aspect of the plot.

Slowly a plan took shape. The Colourful Cottage was then still redolent of its incarnation as the cider barn bar or young farmers' social club. Murky and smelly, with fake black painted beams falling off the ceiling, decorated with signs to exit and to a tiny toilet or vomitorium. The old cider press was used as a bar across the corner and affixed with beer pumps. The rest had been a farm office, once the home of an enormous early computer which spat out reems of that paper with green stripes all over it and holes punched down both sides, which it was hoped (my friend Nobby Kerton told me all about it) would revolutionise the farm in the 1980s and make it economic. How many such reveries have flowered and expired. However, this room and the bedroom above, reached by an enclosed timber staircase, had Crittall windows and a great deal of H. E. Bates-era charm. At the back the remnants of a grizzly pink kitchen had nothing appealing about them but a large double casement opening on to a patch where there had always been vegetable growing going on. Bounded on the north about 30 metres or yards back by a sheltering wild plum hedge. The soil was deep and untainted. It was here we decided to put the kitchen garden and, after a lot of deliberation, the 'poly-folly', the Keder Greenhouse as it likes to be known, a bubble polytunnel with straight sides and German origins, which we ordered, apoplectic with excitement, in the autumn of 2019 just as *Scent Magic* was published. This northern bit of the garden, under the now overgrown Mirabelle plum trees – which Mr B says will crash down in a gale and should be cut back, but which I just love because their outgrown black limbs finger the wintry sky with blossom – is, in my mind, a very flowery allotment. I want it to be both puritan and functional while at the same time wanting it to look like Giverny. Giverny is one of those nirvanas which we have not yet accessed and which like Ninfa (finally attained after a thirty-five year wait) is bound to be a disappointment. Maybe we will never go and just hold our vision of it where we want it. The kitchen garden is so far from looking like Giverny that we are both secretly in despair. I instituted a no-dig approach which has garnered much scoffing from Mr B. And we made the paths too wide for reasons that were valid but boring and now we will have to right it somehow. Then there is the 'pool' garden behind the potting shed and Benton End. For this we have planning permission to make a small walled garden: we have the bricks but neither money nor time to build the walls. Possibly we will put them up bit by bit, me the mate, handing each brick to Mr B.

Benton End is the corner to which we all gravitated carrying our chairs that first spring. It was already partly paved, a natural sitting place, snuck in the elbow of the only wall in the garden. Then we planted the iris rhizomes we had brought with us from Trematon. Then we added some Benton irises from a nursery near Wells, and before we knew it we were making iris beds all the way down the third parallel path going west. The orchard comes beyond on the western boundary, helping the garden shelter from the prevailing wind, and more orchard is now planted on the eastern boundary, this time delicious things, plums and gages rather than bitter cider apples.

At the opposite end to Benton End is the very important hazelnut tree which is the centre of a kind of clique of planting. It started as a mothers' union huddle – hazel and friends: bay, holly, cherry, and that exotic *Parottia persica*, sitting and chatting on the edge of the churchyard. This group formed a natural punctuation point on the edge of which, when we had removed a belt of leylandii, we planted a yew hedge to make our boundary with the church. Mr B would say right from the start that he loved the multi-stemmed hazel and would make it the pivotal point of a path from the front drive to the orchard whose cross axis would be centred on the church's bell tower. He has quietly conjured a winter garden and fernery without really a blink of an eye or any help or interference from me. It just feels right and like it was ever there. It came naturally, completely, and will expand and continue. One of the difficult things about this flat billiard table of a plot was that, while there is something we all love about those slightly unloved bits of garden which come into their own in the winter, it was hard to find such a place here, or even a jumping off point. But Mr B has done it, for the nuttery now hangs off the yew allée and then there is more shrubbery and winter treats between this and the drive.

The rose garden hangs off the north side of the nuttery. I am anxious about it because it has turned out so conventional. It will have to be worked on. The shape was determined by the geometry that was required when the hedging and planning began to solidify. Having fought to retain the huge espalier apple tree which pairs up with the huge old espalier 'Doyenne du Comice' pear tree (about which there was less discussion of destruction), the rose garden garden works well on plan. We just have to get the planting right. The apple unfortunately has very early, very small and very tasteless apples, and is most awkwardly placed, so its head was on the chopping block with Mr B from the beginning. Once the 'dig for Covid' garden described in the next chapter was dismantled – potatoes and onions pop up everywhere still – it seems to have been granted a stay of execution and I think it works very well. Luckily for this tree it sits among a swathe of surviving *Iris tuberosa* (formerly *Hermodactylus tuberosus*), the black widow or snake's head iris, which flowers in February and which we have never succeeded in getting to flourish in any of our gardens. This colony could be moved, says Mr B, along with the apple tree, but he did not quite dare to push it, and I think they are all very much at home now in the new layout. They give it gravitas. Both these venerable espaliers have been hard pruned and are thriving. So too the cider orchard, which was draping itself, bowing down to the ground. Apples seem to be notoriously bad rooters, always falling about like drunken farmers, but more curious to me is their biennial nature. These French cider apples, at least, have one year on and one year off when the blossom and fruit are minimal. Fergus Dowding says if you foliar feed in August they will flower well every year, but I rather like this rhythm of expectation and let down. We have pruned as best we can, raising the crown and taking out the dead, opening up to let the air in. They look much better loved and you can see under them so that the mid-ground when you look west is now a strip of electric green pasture, like a swoosh of Howard Hodgkin saturated paint.

* * *

De-suburbanisation can be the first thing you need to do; certainly at Hanham it was, and here at Ashington too. The east courtyard, which lies behind the house and between it and Colourful Cottage, is a wonderful space with three sides of Hamstone dominated by two towering chimneys. The well has been uncovered here and, in my head, it is to be more of a drying yard. Mr B would have more plants than I would. He tore out the offending sickly Kanzan cherry with his John Deere tractor in week one. Then he bulldozed the cherub pond and fountain, crazy paving, and the butter-coloured kerria with his usual confidence. And he was right. (Maybe this is the title of his biography. His autobiography was always going to be: *I know I am right about this*.)

The back (north) field is annoying. It comprises half the land we bought with the house and, on the face of it, could just as well have been looked after by the grazing dairy herd and not troubled us. But it was no good for that, which is why it was sold with the manor and not the farm. In the 1889 ordinance survey, one hundred years before Historical Child was born, it shows as another bit of the patchwork of orchards that prettily litter this map, a litany of loss. These orchards were part of a matrix of rural life, preserving fruit and vegetables and managing to get through winter. Nobby Kerton, our friend and neighbour in Chilton Cantelo, confirms the severe hardship, the cold, the mud, the almost brutal world of survival that shows in the old photos we have from that time. In the vegetable garden were only staple cabbages and potatoes and a small aluminium greenhouse for tomatoes. Nobby is the warmest, kindest, most positive and polite man I have met in my entire life, a ray of sunshine; mention him to anyone round about and an immediate glow of warmth pervades the conversation. Perhaps all that toil and triumph bred him so. There was cider for comfort and for vinegar. Everyone needed their cider for the joy and relief it brought to a life of boring survival. Such a gentleman and such a countryman, Nobby has taken my hand often and taken me to his youthful days just after the war, when the Cox family – Mr and Mrs and a daughter always called 'Bun' – were the farmers at Ashington, and he would walk over here across the Yeo to blag some ham from Mrs Cox. His eyes are aflame recalling the cider barrels lined up in deep gloom in what is now my studio, and hanging above them, whole hams, blue-velvet-coated with mould. 'But if she gave you some of that orchard-fed pork – she sliced through that electric coat of mould and into the pink flesh – aw, it was sweet as a nut.' Never tasted finer, he says. His own farmhouse is proper, with a cider cellar in a semi-basement filled with bats and all the paraphernalia of cider making – which he does religiously, endless tasting and sipping, collecting loads of apples from his orchards in his pickup, demonstrating at the Sherborne show.

The north field is almost moated; it has a ditch on three sides and the Mirabelle plums on the south behind Colourful Cottage. In the 1970s the Sandemans got grants to put up asbestos barns here, and to the east they put up a big new milking parlour. Photos of this survive and make it look like the film *Witness*, only not as beautiful. Everyone looks elated by the shiny steels of the new parlour, paid for by the European Economic Community: progress and provision. But whatever grantable good reasoning put up all these barns, they lost all purpose, and when Mark and Yseult lived here we wandered about their semi-urban dereliction. This brown field smelled of old grain and rats and bat poo. The bats were abundant and there were several species. Bats, rats, mice, barn owls, foxy smelling. I don't know what the best solution for the buildings would have been, but grinding them up and simply spreading them as hardcore over the back field was not good. In most of the field if you dig, rubble surfaces.

Hopeless for apples, which are bad rooters anyway and could not get their feet into this archaeology. Hopeless for ponies, a wasteland, a dock land with hemlock and tufts of meadow grass. But we can make something of it. This is where I want to put solar panels. The worst part of the land will be where the Logical Child has worked out the solar array will get most light. Around the north and west edges and wherever the ground is undisturbed we have planted native woodland, though this means we will lose the fairy lights of the airfield at Yeovilton on winter nights. We will also lose the distant silhouette of Glastonbury Tor to the north. I was so astonished, when I first realised that, through a gap between Somerton and Castle Cary, you can actually see Glastonbury Tor from our bedroom and the back field that I had to drag the disbelieving Mr B out to see. There it is, the long back view of it, about the size of your fingernail on the horizon. No wonder it was important; its silhouette changes completely depending on which point of the compass you view it from, yet the icon is eternal and powerful. We do seem to have dug out a lot of spoil from inside the house and general drains and things, all part of the shambles which is now driving Mr B so potty. Perhaps we can conjure a mount with a view of the Tor in the field. But my hope is that now that Mr B has got rid of the docks (I help in the harvest before they seed every year), the poor quality of the ground will make for a fine sward and a good impoverished but limey medium for certain wild flowers in a golden meadow. It is home to a million voles and field mice, and the barn owl minesweeps it, low and slow, twice daily.

4
Soil & Hedges & Trees

T he computer growls into action and I come upon my
attempt at a 'positive diary' for 30 November 2021. If one is
attempting a 'positive diary', one is clearly feeling negative
and aggrieved. The builders had been in for six months, so
the first entry is 'Andrew and David managed to put in two hearth
stones quite successfully.' It's not much to write home about, but
Andrew and Graham and their ship's company have been brave
souls as they swung steel into the voids that were bedrooms
before loosening the elm beams like teeth from the jaws of
old masonry, revealing more rot and beetle, more atrocious
bodged builders' work than Mr B could have predicted on a bad
night's drinking. Aboard this ship of fools, Andrew Masters is
the Master, master-builder from two miles down the road. Mr
B is Commander and Graham Cattle is Boatswain. Then there
are their sons, various cousins and semi-relations, vagabonds,
journeymen and general pirates. I am their queen, distant and
terrifying. I thought we would be in the house by Christmas – old

story – now it is almost high summer, and our shore is in sight, but some way off. Back to the November diary, and it says that Mr B and Brian, his amanuensis, batman or warrant officer, have found a cache of bulbs, ordered and forgotten. So that will keep them busy for a while. They must have been the tulips, which turned out to be all the wrong colours, and more *Tulipa sylvestris* for the drive. The drive is inundated with these now, and they outshine the fritillaries. I realised too late that fritillaries are best just with cowslips flowering together, and my heart sinks as I cannot see how anyone sane would be able to dig up all the sylvestris and replant them. They would have to be in flower or just over so that you could see where they were – and the effort, and then the replanting. But I have a feeling it might have to be done. At Trematon we inherited a lot of trumpet-blaring daffodils which I was happy to pick to bring cheer into the house, thus toning down to something more restful the spring scene outside. But Mr B chose to methodically dig them up and root them out for good.

Again back to the positive diary. I only managed three days. One of which mentions the happy fact that it was not raining. Two years before, in November 2019, our first autumn, the rain, you may remember, was biblical. There seems with climate change to be a monsoon moment developing, low deluging skies, around November and December, another perhaps in August (I feel it coming after this the driest of springs). That November the rain was so relentless that I convinced myself it would never let up, that this was the new normal. This is the new reality, I can remember thinking then. This is what climate change means. Not some champagne-growing Elysium for the South Downs, but flash floods in Cornwall and localised violent storms leaving bits of Scotland powerless for more than a week. I do think this is climate change; it means the seasons and the flow of things are all wrong, even in this blessed Scepter'd Isle. It means drought, followed by deluge, and nasty easterly winds in spring. And we are the lucky ones. Positivity is essential, but hard to keep topped up. Yseult had warned us to buy a four-by-four for the floods at Mudford. Opposite Parsonage Farm, by the bridge on the river Yeo, the men in hi-viz are never absent, always tinkering around in some concrete bunker. The uprising of the river brings with it, or certainly did in the past, lots of the fertile alluvial components of our deep soil. So excellent that potatoes were once grown commercially here, and they pumped water up from the river to irrigate them. It is useful, if you like gardening, to find out what the soil is like in your plot. Everywhere in the grass here the mole hills attest to the rich plenty of the earth and its worms, indicating a soil in good heart. Up the hill it is a yellow soil, acid enough for azaleas and blue hydrangeas to grow, called Yeovil Sands. This is a sort of unformed Hamstone. But here the soil is dark brown and about two feet deep above a free-draining subsoil which is full of toffee-coloured flint pebbles. We have been meaning to get the pH tested, but it seems neutral and productive. Despite the soil's being so free-draining, the water table is dangerously high, hence no cellar in this house, and when we began to dig down inside for the structural work and insulating under the stone floor (at the same time we found the Elizabethan slabs beneath the floor – huge, and pretty much perfect), we saw the glistening meniscus of water forming just about 2½ feet below the finished floor level. Master and Commander have worked out a system of French drains to keep this lower whenever possible, but when we see the pond edging towards us it means that beneath our feet the water is coming up to greet also.

Healthy soil is 50 per cent air, space, a void, or many voids filled with gases. The rest is largely water. The soufflé that you might be lucky enough to find in your garden has been very slowly arrived at, and I think it might help if we thought about it more as the living thing that it is. As we now think of the gut as containing a living biome, so too our soil, which needs feeding and nurturing, and we should attend to the soil more than the plants. We should start with soil, and we should to be amazed by its wealth and complexity. The underworld is a miracle that we barely grasp. The era of synthetic soluble plant foods – delivering nitrogen and potash – needs to give way to an understanding of soil health. Soil works as an organism, and it is filled with organisms, particularly mycorrhizal fungi, which metabolise pollutants, oil, heavy metals and nitrogen run-off into stable humus.

At Ashington there was no tillage in the garden for possibly thirty years. In the Covid spring of 2020, we rushed to open up beds and plant onions, potatoes, cavolo nero and kale. We bought clear plastic sort-of-cupboards to keep our seedlings from etiolating and later for growing on tomatoes so that they would ripen. For once we had time to tend them properly. In this 'virgin bower' the normally rampant pests and diseases kept away. The broad beans were not coated with blackfly nor was there canker or clubroot. Tillage increases soil respiration, releasing carbon dioxide into the air. In the garden I think it is easier and less expensive to mulch and to leave less done, less tidying up, less digging, let the skeletal forms overwinter and it is better for everything. At least the fashion for prairie planting has instilled in everyone a love of skeleton plants and wands in the off season, and time to enjoy their stillness, their movement and their palette of straw. Mr B claims to love digging and is very scoffing about No-Dig. Mrs B, on the other hand, took the office and friends to Charles Dowding's course on the No-Dig growing principle, which is held nearby, and everybody loved it. Like an evangelistic meeting we were all converted by the preacher's enthusiasm. The vegetable garden here was No-Dig, laid down with cardboard and smothered with council waste mulch. It seems pretty excellent, but then so does the rest of the Dig-Dig garden at the moment. We always mulch our flower beds madly because we don't have much labour to weed in summer and it keeps things cool and moist, my favourite word. But Mr Dowding is really only interested in vegetables, and his fruit trees have done remarkably well. What he does just goes to prove beyond doubt that soil is king.

My big bugbear has always been the problem of compaction, which is almost always the result of changing or building anything in the garden. As garden designers, we are so often handed over a building site at the end of three years of beeping and reversing machinery trundling like tanks over everywhere, completely without regard for the soil. I worry about compaction constantly, because it is alarmingly difficult to reverse and must therefore be avoided at all costs. I worry whenever we bring in a machine here. Of course, you have to do certain things, like dig drains, but up until the 1950s everything was done by hand or horse. Small feet, limited damage, not like these tons of metal and their big grabs and arms. I think it is the root of so many beginners' disillusionment with gardening. I see the house-building companies trashing a field and then fencing in plots of compacted earth and calling it the 'garden'. Nothing grows there, not even the turf they chuck on it. The chances of anything doing well in such conditions without a lot of preparation and restorative effort are minimal. Charles Dowding would suggest that you could cover this beaten-up land with compost, and it would naturally regenerate. I am sure it would help, but if you are starting with a really trashed plot, I tend to think you might need a bit more than a copper spade and a load of council compost, wonderful though these things are. Mr B would not advocate hiring a rotavator either. Rotavators are great if you already have good tilth, but on poor ground they do two things you don't want. They chop all the weeds like docks and ground elder, should they be present, into a thousand little cuttings, all of which will grow with renewed vigour. And they create what is called a 'pan' just beneath where they reach with their chopping iron fingers. You get a lovely tilth on top. Looks great. But only so far and beneath that they tend to leave a compacted layer, like baked dough, through which nothing will grow.

I realise more and more that this is so often an underlying problem. I have begun to note the feel of the earth beneath my feet. I am learning from it; you can feel when it is unforgiving and airless. Without air and worms, without the threads of roots and fungi, the soil is dying or dead and very hard to revive. Take time and you often notice that even grass is not growing well. I give an example. We finally got to the Garden of Ninfa, south of Rome, in 2017. We were lucky to be allowed in after hours, but as we arrived coach upon coach departed crammed with happy visitors. And we all want to visit things. However, this garden is half private and half open to the throngs for a short period of the year. And what is fascinating is the obvious and visible difference in plant health and vitality in the two halves. Flourishing still in the private half, tired-looking in the rest of the garden. The problem of this relentless footfall has been recognised and steps were being taken to limit visitors to paths enclosed by lavender hedges and borders, but these impinge on the magic of the garden and mean that sadly everyone is cooped up and not able to enjoy the whole as the immersive experience which was intended. Ashington will never suffer like this, but anyone starting a garden or taking on a garden should try to examine the state of the soil all around that garden and try to do the best to revivify and restore it. This is the place to start once you have your layout and paths and so forth. Compost from the council is an excellent way to start and, better still, making your own once you get going.

* * *

When we set out the structure of a garden we need verticals, we need to make 'rooms' and develop surprise, and above all, I have come to realise, safety. It is cosier not to be placed looking across a runway of lawn, as if on the deck of some aircraft carrier, although this can be magnificent as at Hanham Court where the runway of grass ended in a distant view framed with trees either side like a stage set. Tower blocks on pilotis in Elysian Fields of grass are intimidating, however beautiful. We are cave dwellers at heart, and we crave shelter. Plants also crave shelter more often than not – walls and the filtering shelter of hedges. I am a big fan of the much-maligned privet hedge – fast and furious and always green. Mr B does not agree. He is right that this quickness becomes a chore, always needing to be trimmed unless you let it run free and flower. Wild privet has always been invaluable planting in covers and copses and woodland for its winter presence and hence warming wind-filtering qualities. Some of our best ancient woodland, and not so ancient, was created as shelter for shooting game and you will find these places – sadly now devastated by ash dieback – are most often underplanted with holly, box and privet. Privet being far and away the fastest of these to establish, but the least handsome. I don't really mind a hedge of any plant, so long as it's green and not variegated or purple.

The yew tree is Mr B's greatest friend. He loves them, saying they provide grace and stability, from the Pilgrim's Way, where they thrive high upon the Downs in pure chalk (they do not like wet feet), to the bubbly hedges at Montacute or Corsham Court, both of which have been living sculpture for hundreds of years. They are the oldest standing trees in Britain – the Fortingall yew in Perthshire is between two and three thousand years old. As large trees they can also provide a slightly edgy shade; the dry gloom of centuries lies beneath them, powerful, even slightly evil. It is good to have a note of frisson in a garden, like a grotto or cave or dangerous water. Variations of mood, shafts of strange light, something magic like the silvery moss beneath groves of beech trees. But there is something timeless and tranquil about a yew hedge. They don't really take all that long to grow. Like anything, if you can reduce the competition and up the health with foliar seaweed feed, blood fish and bone in spring round the bottom, and a mulch, they will return the compliment. When you are young things grow faster. Here at Ashington we have cheated by planting surprisingly big hedging, as well as the terrifically cheating big beehives of yew topiary. Both of which were a major indulgence. But we may not have long to enjoy them, so we feel we are in a hurry. Not the best recipe for a great garden, but it's not an overriding feeling, just a niggle. Beech hedging is faster and can be bought bigger for less, but it is not a particular favourite of Mr B's or mine, although the rusty colour it keeps in winter would be good here with the stone. Mr B is quite circumspect in what he will choose to make a hedge with, and quite disciplined. While he may like the idea of hedges of rugosas or rubiginosa roses, he rarely specifies such in our designs. He prefers to stay on the safe and classic path and not wander off into botany. A camellia hedge can be a beautiful thing, and I have plans for the solar-farm-hiding which involve different types of ribes and raspberries. But Mr B will not like them. We opted without much thought and no argument for lavender hedges running out to the west because they smell of madrigals and hot, stony places.

We wanted old English lavender, large and late flowering, and by some miracle in March 2020 we trawled the B&Qs of Somerset buying lavender plants, nameless but with a big healthy-looking leaf and vigour. It has turned out to be just like old English, infinitely more pleasing than the varieties we have used to fill in (where my nasturtiums had strangled the best B&Q variety). Rosemary is more of a favourite; being so early into flower it is the bearer of hope as well as the keeper of memories, but it is plagued with problems and pests. An informal hedgerow of wintersweet along with a puffing cloud hedge of lilac have always been part of Mr B's mythology.

Hedges don't have to be straight; they can have wavy tops, be clouds, be battered or crinkle-crankle, but yew, box, beech and hornbeam are the most classic and rewarding plants to use for hedging, and just setting out the small plants in rows will give you a lift. Louise Dowding keeps all her box topiary disease-free by biweekly sprays of neem oil and seaweed feed. Luckily for us there was not only the Irish sentinel yew at the front of the house but a good few carriages of a hedge of yew like a train separating front drive from proper garden. Although they hate wet feet, yews need help to make adventitious roots and get going, so even here we insured ourselves when planting the big beehives with a drip-line system which we used for the first two years when it was really dry. Mr B loves topiary clipped against a wall; even a well-clipped cotoneaster can be a satisfying thing against a wall. He loves espaliers and pleaching and all kinds of torturing. Topiary does what ornamental and architectural things do; you can make houses or vistas, providing verticality, a shape, a story, a dialogue. We knew it was what we needed here. Mr B calls it 'grounding'. There is the historical precedent. First time round it was Jacobean gardens and then the nineteenth-century Jacobean revival gardens that everyone finds full of peace and fulfilment: Packwood, Levens Hall, Earlshall in Fife. But simple shapes cross timelines, and clipped forms are equally part of the finest modern gardens. The extraordinary Belgian nursery Solitaire fashioned a series of 'rock' or 'boulder' shapes in box some years ago, which were stupendous. Gardens need verticals, and they need curves against straight lines, and clipped forms are one way of introducing these. Margery Fish and Walter chose blue cypresses to achieve a vertical avenue at East Lambrook. Horrible plants, but they look good in a black and white photograph.

Hedges are the quickest way to set out structure and shelter, and walls too, but we will come to them. On the eastern boundary here, where the farmyard was and where two lonely tin barns are hanging on beyond our boundary, we are hedging our bets and compromising with one another. I am mad keen to keep the only view in the place, looking east towards Windmill Hill and Patson Hill. Mr B calls them the Ngong Hills, though a bitter east wind blows from there, especially in spring it seems. Who knows what might happen to the barns? At present there is boring close-boarded fence, and as we don't want too definite an edge to things here – we want it to look like we own more land, further out – we have planted a medley of things: honeysuckle, elder, hawthorn, willows, buddleias, wild and rambling roses. Maybe I will get some privet in and wild pears and apples. This choice of plants needs to hide the fence but not the view, not grow too tall or require too much cutting. This fence I found curiously offensive. Its close-boarded guarded attitude was not rural. The whole place was suffering from that attitude called bastard farmer: concreted over cobbles, bulldozed asbestos barns, mangled cattle troughs. First, I asked Robert, man of oak, to cut the fence in half so that I could see the Ngong Hills. Now it is slowly disappearing behind the planting we have got going there.

Mr B's confidence and determination are most admirable but one person's necessary reorganisation is bound to be another person's trashing something affectionately familiar. Being offensive without realising it is something we are all quite capable of, and in the patchwork of modern back-garden life, it is difficult to always see everyone's point of view. I think our neighbours were not a little shocked by the 'Tornado' rabbit- and badger-proof fencing that Mr B insisted he could not garden without. He was right about this, but it was a tricky moment, as our delightful neighbours and their even more delightful children had had a free run of the place while it was unoccupied. The shiny tight-gridded 'Tornado' wire really is badger proof, but it looks, our neighbours told us jokingly but with feeling, like Donald Trump's Mexican Wall. We wanted the children to continue playing in the orchard, but I think we scared them off. Perhaps they will be assuaged by the fact that having a badger-proof garden means we can adopt hedgehogs, and I feel the birds enjoy the fact that the fence is a bit too much trouble for the village cats to negotiate.

On the eight acres, then, is not a single oak or beech tree. The lime trees are from the Sandemans' 1970s planting along with some Norway maples and an Indian horse chestnut. The Lombardy poplar is older, I would think. The sycamore between us and the church we had massacred immediately in order to get light into the drive. It will recover and spread out its lifted crown in time. Mr B and I love sycamores, especially where they thrive and grow huge in Yorkshire, East Lothian and Devon. I have just read that a mature sycamore tree provides as much nectar and pollen as six acres of meadow. Although I feel it is not quite as simple as that because it depends *what* invertebrate is the beneficiary. In my childhood they were rather despised by the old ladies of our village for being full of hoverflies and gnats, so they must be good hunting grounds for things further up the food chain such as bats and swallows.

5
Stoned

What we needed here at Ashington were paths. Paths almost asked to get laid, seemed fundamental to making a design, a form of drawing. First came the path outside my old office on the west side of what would be the great hall. This headed straight out like a bullet through the orchard and west with the night. Outside the door you need to turn right or left, but for now there is a scrap of leylandii sprouting brambles and a yew which prevent your getting round to the front of the house by turning left. I was surprised Mr B did not have these out in the very early days, yet he still seems reluctant, uncertain of quite how we should treat this corner. It will be resolved. To the right is the holy of holies, the part of the house we all love the best, the west-facing biscuit-coloured wall punched out with Gothic tracery which on summer evenings, after a basking in afternoon heat, radiates the day's warmth back at you, like a storage heater. It was self-evident that this was where you would gather to eat and drink outside, near enough the kitchen. When we design, we are trying to hit the spot between clutter and proportion. There is a right way where the size of garden, the dimensions of the house, the width of the path and terrace come together into perfect cohesion. That is what we hope for. Here my feeling is that the terrace is not quite wide enough. In order to make it so we would have to unpick roses and rosemary and lavender of the permanent planting and then the sweet pea tepees and the matthiola, which will run out of steam shortly anyway. Mr B knows I am right about this, but sighs at the backwards motion required. I understand. But eventually, in my head it is wider, and it is paved. Immediately we came here we put down Type 1 (the grey stuff builders use for everything, including the base material for roads and paths, up to 40 millimetre down in size, made of crushed limestone usually, and sometimes called 'chippings to dust') followed by Hills Cotswold path gravel, which is a self-binding gravel, smaller scale – 14 millimetres down – which is whacker plated or rolled to compact it beautifully and then dusted with a 6 millimetre pea gravel very thinly. The top layer needs to be topped up occasionally and can be rolled into the self-binding part.

Limestone is at the heart of much of the geology of the British Isles and hence also the architecture and the appearance of them. Of course, there are many and large parts which are on chalk, perhaps with flint, in the south and east, and there is the granite that underlies Devon and Cornwall and much of Scotland, but here at Ashington we are on a golden counterpane of limestone, threaded with 'blue lias', which is a generally inferior grey colour. Ashington, like all the villages round about, has a mix of building materials: lias, Hamstone, brick. Hamstone has always been highly prized and reclamation is an old game. The walls of Muchelney Abbey were mostly stolen by locals, using it like a quarry, within a hundred years of its dissolution. Montecute House was probably built using the stone from a Cluniac monastery previously there, but also had a whole back corridor and façade added to it in the eighteenth century, purchased at the demolition of nearby Clifton Maybank Hall. When Ashington was remodelled and reduced, it appears that, naturally, much of the salvage was used as building material. Brick walls generally welcome plants although their fullness of colour makes the choice of flowering plant more complicated, I think. Lias walls are so grey they welcome any colour, but I think are particularly enhanced by yellows and lilacs. The Hamstone walls here are so lichenous and such a miraculous colour that it seems a crime to cover them with anything. Would you want to muss this perfection with even just roses? We are agreed, no mish-mash of messy climbers here. That is for the bad bits of crumbly lias. Jasmine for all north-facing walls, usually with roses 'Albéric Barbier' and 'Madame Alfred Carrière' – both good at shade. But a single type of rose perhaps? It happened this spring. Mr B snuck in a couple of roses. 'Climbing Lady Hillingdon' is now lurking at the foot of the west wall. It looks great at Lytes Cary where it is dainty and not at all overwhelming. It is interesting, the balance of habit and planting which I feel needs more than my lifetime to learn. How plants grow, their habit, is not something you can estimate from a book. But it is really important. Roses particularly behave in such differing ways. The point here is to choose something which is just a wisp of colour and form, so as to decorate something already perfect. Like a veil. It is the same with massed bulb planting: the difference is all in the spread and intensity of the planting. I visited a small dell filled with indigenous daffodils in Dorset last spring, and could not believe the musical timing of the natural distribution and density of their self-spreading. It was a lesson. At the foot of the wall a bed was dug out for crinums from Avon Bulbs. But on second thoughts the prospect of their scruffiness held us back, and they have a new home where this failing doesn't matter, behind the pantry. Brian having gone to all the trouble to dig out a serious bed here and then hide it again under hoggin, something needs to go there. Together we are thinking just agapanthus perhaps. It is tricky, and hard to undo something which has taken such a lot of effort.

From the terrace, the paths begin naturally to emanate and radiate. North towards the potting shed where the path goes through the building, you can see beyond into the yet-to-be-made walled garden. At the junction between terrace and the stair tower a second, wide path heads west, companion to the one from my old office, the west door. They form the jambs of an H-shaped court, with the lawn in the middle, the solid heart of the whole. We debated whether putting the whole thing down to gravel might be more like an eighteenth-century Jan Kipp engraving of an early garden, and the pull of the Edwardian Jacobean revival drew us in that direction also. Historical Child is less bothered by these nuances: he likes what he likes, and this is our overriding principle in everything, but we both have heads full of precedents and examples, too many notes and photos sloshing about. For the moment, the simple lawn has won and no formal fenced finale has intervened, although I yearn for something like the long-gone oak balustrade at Owlpen – in fact the whole mood of that Tudor manor house – or Kelmscott Manor, where William Morris lived, is something we want to channel, in a small way, if we can. Do we need a division between the *hortus conclusus* and the orchard? Two pairs of oak posts with balls suggest it, delineating the vestige of some former formality. Do we need to open up the orchard, removing or moving apple trees to create a sweeping vista west to the polder and the Constable-like view? The blossom was so good this year, why mess with a bower of bliss?

The walled garden behind the go-through potting shed is still way out in the realms of fantasy. We have planning permission for it, and a swimming pool of some ornamental sort, but no dollar. The garden walls we fantasise about are a ruddy red brick. One of the most enchanting architectural occurrences round here, at Hinton Farm Red Barn and at Parsonage Farm Mudford, is the juxtaposition of Hamstone with Georgian red brick. The brick must have come up the Parrett from Bridgewater and, along with the terracotta roof tiles, begun to transform the look of Somerset by the end of the eighteenth century. From architecture made simply from lias and Hamstone with mostly thatch and some stone roofing, a new look, rather cheerier and ruddy in combination with all those materials, gives the medley we love today. Farm buildings went up fast and furious; early stone farmhouses were gradually huddled with quickly built byres and barns with a warm charm and slate or the pantile roofs, which are such a feature of the countryside within haulage distance of Bridgewater where they were first made. We have our Red Barn, which was a drive-through for hay wains or carts of some kind, open-ended like an agricultural *porte cochère*. Next to it is a brick outhouse, the curiosity I call the 'Signalman's' because it has that aura of early railway architecture and an outside staircase. (It also contains all the WiFi and Starlink satellite operational kit and is the centre of signals ops run by Logical Child, who saved me from the nervous breakdown that was almost brought on by rural Internet. With ingenuity and patience he connected us through satellite at some considerable expense. Superfast fibre broadband is coming. Super slowly.)

The house would have been surrounded by a clutter of farm buildings and it would be great to regenerate that somehow. The planners, however, did not like even the corrugated iron barn that we applied for and on which we proposed to put solar panels where no one could see them. In order to get on with the renewable agenda we had to back down and put them in the back field. Late at night Mr B and I speculate what earlier stables and barns were here *ante ignem*. There is no record, not archaeological nor legal, of what outbuildings there were here before the nineteenth century. The imagined walled garden, then, has only two walls for monetary reasons and also to keep the connection with the orchard. On our planning application there is one wall to the east and one to the north: west facing and south facing, the best for horticulture. There is a north-facing side to the wall already here which faces south in the *hortus conclusus*, the flower garden, and through which we have broken an aperture or gateway which prolongs the (church's) bell tower axis all the way to the Mirabelle plums on the north. The twenty-three pieces of topiary, the yew beehives that we planted in fear of our imminent demises, dominate the whole garden, as intended. We both think it works, no matter what else doesn't. The idea of the pool, then, is to be a traditional tank of water on this axis and behind it a simple lean-to byre or shelter. Around this pool I see an opportunity to use up all the broken bits of blue lias paving that were lying around the place and grow plants in the resultant 'crazy' paving. Yuck, says Mr B.

Blue lias was the preferred flooring flag of these parts in past centuries. It is a rather rubbish stone, grey as concrete; as a walling stone rather depressing, although lovely if lichen covered. It has the attribute of laminating in thick flat layers, ideal for paving, and is also used vertically around here as a sort of stone fence. Excellent for pigsties, this stone fencing was quick to put up and apt to fall down. At Ashington in the mid-twentieth century there were miles of it, like broken teeth. The golden limestone down here is not generally good for paving, unlike like Bath and Cotswold stone, and farmhouses from Radstock to Burton Bradstock generally had blue lias floors everywhere on all the lower stories but the parlour. This is important stuff because it informs the local look of a place and hence the feel. The granite and slate floors of Devon and Cornwall are entirely different in feeling. York stone is the ideal outdoor paving because it is non-slip, consistent and beautiful, and so it has been used all over the country for centuries wherever it was reasonably possible to transport it, so down the east coast to Norfolk and as far as Kent. We use it all the time at work, but we would not want it here, ideally. This kind of lost subtlety may seem increasingly pointless, but it makes all the difference to us. Brick paths can be lovely also, and they feel right in many places and are practical and economical if you take time to lay them properly, without making a Victoria sponge of mortar joints. It is good to vary textures and hues; Arts and Crafts gardens expressed this admirably, but we think we are aspiring here to reduce the sense of artifice. My paltry advice on paving and bricklaying, floor-making and wall-making, is to try to avoid what all builders do these days, which is to use masses of mortar as glue or cream filling. It makes their life easier, is much less skilled and the resulting look is horrible. Specifiers and engineers and builders like to lay a great raft of concrete and lay garden paths and paving on to it. Clearly, nothing will grow in such a set-up, and this is the aim of the engineers and the consequence of this litigious life. The aim is that nothing will change, develop character, move or respond to heat and cold and the earth beneath. Lime mortar walls not only breathe but move without detriment to their fundamental soundness. We like things that move and get a bit wonky. We like a bit of wonk. Obviously, it doesn't help if you are making a pond or a swimming pool. I developed grey hair first over making a swimming pool on top of a hill with a high water table. Because the waterproof render kept cracking, we had to install a pump *outside* the pool walls to keep the pressure off from the high water outside the pool until it was filled with water to balance it inside. Some people hate nails on blackboards; I hate wide jointing on paving or tiles or bricks or anything. Lay your paving on compacted Type 1 or a self-binding hoggin and plants will get their roots down through it; they will lift it and give it the undulations and charm that you have often admired elsewhere (in a Margery-Fish kind of way). The bottom substrate can be anything – stuff you are taking to the tip like clinker or broken bricks, as long as they are really well compacted and cannot escape to the visual layer on top. The problem with recycled substrates, and scalpings also, is that if you do have to dig up a path they come to the top and somehow you never get rid of them. Making your own cobbles using flints, pebbles from a stream or ditch, or bits of rock and stone that you find when you dig up your garden is most satisfying and rewarding. But it needs to be done in courses, and with finesse. When I joke with Mr B about crazy paving, we both know I don't mean broken concrete paviours.

It is a dream to behold the fine old pebble work in those places where stone for paving was not abundant; we are always admiring that found in the paths to Devon churches. Before gross tourism and trade, path-layers used what stones they had with experience and wisdom, tightly worked together, as flat-sided as possible with some long in the tooth so as to peg the whole into the ground beneath. No gluing together with Portland cement. Just the same as good walling and paving. A minimum of lime to give a bit of hold and for levelling. It is almost a lost art but there to be discovered with a spirit level and patience. Grotto-making, which we used to do, was all like this, but there are only so many grottos anyone wants or wants to make. The key with all these things is materials: finding them through looking with purpose, and using them well. Well-made paths and paving can take lots of wear and will even improve with age. At Trent church near here there is a sign: 'All Persons are requested to take off Pattens and Cloggs before entering the Church.' But here at Ashington, when the hall and kitchen are back to their lias stone floors, the one idea is that you don't have to take your shoes or boots off at the door. Perhaps the reclaimed foot scrapers that are lying about longing for a home will come in handy. Paths in a garden are fundamental to the design and the use of the garden once you have made it. Our favoured path material, which is relatively cheap and easy to lay, is self-binding gravel or hoggin. It may have been owing to European directives that when we started making gardens all gravel was washed in the quarry. You had to beg them to sell you 'as dug' ballast, the stuff as it came out of the ground, maybe screened to a chosen size limit. They almost gave the stuff away laughing. Breedon gravel appeared on the scene at some point; it was expensive but 'self-binding' and you could whack it down like a French boules court, and put fine pea gravel on top to reduce the dust coming over the threshold. A revolution has spread, and many places now offer self-binding gravel; screened to 14 millimetres down is what we recommend, in about a 100 millimetre thick layer. Mr B and I really like gravel. Another endearing attribute is the wonderful colour, a golden snowfall. A gravel path reflects light back up into the windows of a house. Paving tends to go dark with age and gravel does not. This can be invaluable in dark courtyards and basement areas. Grass is green and green is great, but it is also light absorbing. Gravel means plants can tumble out of bed and loll about over the path, seeding themselves everywhere. Weeding is weeding. It has got to be done and weeding gravel is not so bad. We think of our paths as an extension of the flower bed. This doesn't work with grass paths, and grass paths are always needing mowing and edging. There is a problem where golden is not the local colour. My heart sank at having to live in Cornwall with its grey crushed granite drives and paths. Often in the past these paths were made of tiny river and beach pebbles of many hues. There was no industrially crushed stuff to use. Mr B finds it 'creamtorial' (crematorium-like), as they might say in Bristol. The pink granite crush can be quite pretty but seems harder to get hold of now. At Trematon we imported our drive material, much to the horror of locals. We used a small sharp flint called Chardstock from near Chard in the far west of Somerset – almost Devon. The colour really cheered us up. We are always on the hunt for new sources and materials.

* * *

Walls are the backbone of this garden even though they are few, other than those which form the house itself. There are the red brick walls of the Signalman's and the Red Barn. Red brick has always been a bit of challenge to me. I think getting the colour of flowers right with stone or brick can be difficult, but on the whole we don't tend to agonise about these things but just plant what we like. I so admire people who take infinite care to get things right, but for me there is no right. Things sometimes look a bit wrong. Maybe one colour sets your teeth on edge with another. However, in the end, greyed wood, old brick, stone and flint seem really to go with anything. A flint wall with a shocking pink rose like 'Complicata' against it is somehow very appealing. Colour can sing, and life can be very grey. I suppose this is why people take such infinite care, but for me – maybe less for Mr B – planting is like a party; the more you throw at it the better it swings (unless you are doing a theme – white, or blue, or clashing colours, which I love).

We have a south-facing wall that extends either side of the potting shed. Here was the old espalier pear, barely rescuable but still there. Mr B planted *Rosa* 'The Garland' the minute he got here, grasping the opportunity of a quickly made flower bed at the bottom of the wall and a chance place to get a few things going without pressure of disturbance and change. This rambling rose has rewarded his indulgence and care by reaching the eaves in three years and spreading lavishly along in all directions. There are still the hollyhocks and lupins we plunged in there and opposite at the foot of the north wall of our bedroom. This wall was partly rebuilt in the hot summer of 1976, when they re-roofed Ashington with Cotswold stone tiles and built the top half of this gable end again. It must have been in a bad way. The idea is to cover it with the roses 'Madame Alfred Carrière' and 'Albéric Barbier' because they seem to thrive and flower on a north wall.

Ever since I can remember, Mr B and I have had a yen for clipped green shapes and forms on walls. They feature in David Hicks's book. Ivy trellis and even pyracantha espaliers are incredible. The satisfaction of a simple idea expressed well. At Seend Manor we did an architecturally based arcade of clipped ivy against brick walls, which they keep with Japanese precision. Conversely, Mr B and I are subconsciously wary of clothing walls in climbers which get a bit hairy or matted. I simply adore the flowers and smell of *Clematis armandii* but I have had to concede that it needs to go in a well-chosen spot because its massive thuggish leaves are not good the rest of the year. Perhaps plant it to hide a north wall where the bins are or the compost is, and really only see it running fine and flowery along the sunny top of that wall. The Clematis I like are either early or late and small-flowering, the alpinas and viticellas particularly, twining lightly through other things. I love the massive scented tresses of montana types in spring – but again perhaps you don't want that in an important bit of garden, but up a tree by the garage or somewhere. Increasingly I don't want my garden to be a garden centre. I don't want a multitudinous collection of varieties and hybrids. I am probably about to contradict myself. But I think this problem – more an uncomfortable feeling with too many different things – is especially delicate with planting for walls. I like a lot of the same thing: trained fruit, wisteria, jasmine (on the north) even; and Mr B will wince, but I have seen *Elaeagnus* × *ebbingei* trained up the front of a house, all over, and thick as a hedge almost – it looked great. A lot of the same thing, whatever it be. I cannot say it enough. A house cosseted with, say, a banksian rose, especially if it is not so pretty or distinguished a house, is a great thing. And *Rosa banksiae* 'Lutea' can grow like hydra. Maybe the banksian rose would be good camouflage for the wonky bits on the front of this house. Because of the builders and scaffolding and everything going on, Mr B and I have yet to work out the planting here, but the main contenders seems to be banksian roses, wisteria, and *Magnolia grandiflora* maybe with some clipped yew.

Walls lead to buildings. Garden buildings are very important in our lexicon. We like to make places to go, be they tool sheds or banqueting houses, counterpoints to all the planting. We started making oak buildings because it made making buildings possible; it was cheap enough to be feasible, unlike stone. Oak can be fashioned off-site and assembled with little impact or machinery (on the whole). We wanted to do something marvellous at Highgrove and there was barely a budget. We looked to the past, to rustic buildings in gardens and groves, to Thomas Wright at Badminton in the eighteenth century. It seemed to work, and we have developed the idea in all sorts of directions. My favourite shanty that we have made was for catching the end of the day and eating, at Hanham, high at the top of the orchard looking down over the house. Mr B said it was the ugliest building he had ever had a hand in, but it worked. Dachas and rustic fishing huts, by a pool, in an orchard, with a view, up some steps, sunken down or shaken up, with a fire, in a byre, somewhere to eat green eggs and ham; the impulse to go somewhere and hang out or do things is in all of us. In all our gardens too. The man-cave and the shed, the goddam shepherd's hut, the idea of it so pregnant with possibility, so adolescent. These hangouts are generally the place for after work. Here at Ashington the great seduction was the west-facing side of the house and the clear understanding that here we would eat, drink and be merry. This side of the house is cool in the morning. Dew lies glassy on the stone table with intimations of clouds moving across it.

You know those May mornings when you think 'this is the moment … the moment of the year'. For gardeners it is always about to be a moment for something, or it was last week and you missed it. The orchard was never more orchardy and when the dairy herd mob graze in the field behind the garden you can smell their pelts and hear the tearing of turf with bovine teeth. We are still having an argument over whether to extend the vista to the west where they are munching. Whether to open up the orchard by moving some trees and extending the runway lawn.

Really, is this necessary? Mr B and his man friends are convinced the formality should strike out into the polder and poplar-decked landscape. But I am an advocate for the higgledy hidden thing, formality only hinted at, a ghostly imprint of former glory. The yews do this perfectly and that was Mr B's idea entirely. They channel the inner Owlpen Manor. The yews we have planted here already foster finches and collared doves. Pigeons, says Mr B, sounding a bit like my mother, who had an expression she used a lot about my aunt: 'All her Geese are Swans' – by which she meant that her sister exaggerated the talents of her children, her friends and domestic animals. I think she was right to do so; she was positive whereas my mother was always critical and discontented. All my bees are dons. The masonry bees clearly live a very erudite monastic life, reading in their cells in the walls here. But do they lie abed in the morning? There seems no movement, not a hint on this cool sunless side of house in the morning of their afternoon antics, while at the end of the day I sit watching their comings and goings all along the pointing joints, endless tiny portals. We once visited Canons Ashby in Northants and the riddling of holes in the garden walls there left us agog. Centuries of bee activity must have given the National Trust such a headache. But we will have to repoint this side carefully and get 'Glastonbury', as they call him, the builder, to be careful with his lime mortar so as not to disturb this Yemeni city, or the Elastoplast of pink and orange lichen. I look at the young 'Lady Hillingdon' rose at the foot of the wall and wonder if we did the right thing. But the bees will come and go, the radiator stone warming them after dark.

* * *

Terraces and pots go together. Pots beside doors, on your way in, your way out. At Hanham there was such an infestation of grey squirrels that we planted tulips only in pots and put mesh just below the compost surface. Such a discipline is good in a way. A certain amount of tulips in pots is better than sprinkling them everywhere, but the old ones do generally get planted out somewhere, and deep, in the hope they will come back for a bit.

The pots are standard flowerpot-shaped in our garden. We like them plain, undecorated terracotta, but oversized. I mean really big. This has a singular advantage in that it makes the microhabitat work more efficiently – less watering, more growing medium, better plants. Some people have a way with pots: my dad, Mr B – and now Historical Child I think has it too. Not me. But they bravely overstuff and somehow prink and prod all the time to make things look fine. Removing leaves that are annoying as well as the sickly ones. Mr B removes all the large basal leaves from *Nicotiana mutabilis* when he grows it in pots, in order to stop them swamping other things like night-scented stocks hanging over the edge and the broccoli heads of heliotrope in the mid-level, while the nicotiana have wands which shoot up high. When we started gardening it was very difficult to get big pots, and those there were had swags and oranges on them. They were fine. Big pots from Italy were exceptionally expensive and not frost-hardy. Then Jim Keeling at Whichford Pottery changed the game by making exquisite lattice-decorated decent-sized pots that were slightly vase shaped, as pleasing as perfect apple tart. Jim's pots are not only hardy but will last as long as you treat them right. Eventually he made the monumental Great Rollright pot. Still way beyond our means, but for good reason – how they manage to fire something three feet in diameter is anyone's guess – I get excited just looking at them in their hand-thrown glory. Clive Bowen made huge hand-thrown pots in the 1980s which were artworks. Nearby, at Barnstable, C. H. Brannam used to make large flowerpots. Then they made them in China, then everybody made them in China and the Barnstable pottery factory closed. Now we have container-loads of choice but not home-grown.

Mr B's way with pots is to feed and water them assiduously. He cares for them. He remembers them and he takes the change-over from spring to summer planting and the autumn change-back very seriously. We have just done it. I do my assisting bit. Keeping quiet, holding the fork and wheeling away the outcasts as directed, cleaning up at the end. It is a big, messy, military task. Mr B keeps his lilies all winter behind the poly-folly. This year he says they were too long there, on the north side of things, getting etiolated and thinking they were forgotten. I suspect that he always feels this, and that they always recover and bud up once in their rich pots of compost and slow-release fertiliser. Tulips and wallflowers followed by pelargoniums, lilies and some heliotrope, with night-scented stocks like the beards on mussels down the sides. Lilies and pellies come out to play at the end of May. This is the joy of the poly-folly. The brugmansias come out next. There are usually a few experiments, some pots of salvias and *Lantana* 'Calipo Tutti Frutti', sunset shades of hairy and prickly guava-smelling tenderness. Last year everyone seemed to be putting eucomis in pots, to huge architectural effect.

* * *

Finding old things has become a national pastime on the Internet. There is less and less out there to find, but it is fun, especially if you want things to look as they did in 1951. We have things we bought thirty years ago and still have not found a use for. Every time we have moved house I have tried to cull and rationalise, but foot scrapers and greenhouse staging will always carry a potentiality which makes one just hang on to them. Piles of stone, bricks, timber and identifiable lumps are everywhere here. Logical Child asks what I plan for this or that, and I say I don't know but I know there might be a use some day, some place. But judging by some of the thirty-year hangers-on his question is valid. We do use these things in our work, which is a good excuse. They are 'stock'. There is a particular decorative Gothick lintel which I swear has a jinx on it. Helen (who has worked with us for two decades) and I have created buildings around it maybe seven times and always the project does not go ahead. I have a plan to use it here, a good plan, but I wonder if it will happen. Nobody wants to buy it. The real problem with junk is if it needs mending. Mending is a whole other department, one which we are really bad at. Naughty as children with our toys. But on the plus side, a strange or surprising object can make a scheme or inspire a scheme. The capital from a 1930s bank can create its own scene in a woodland setting. Troughs and tanks are invaluable tools for making a garden scene come into its own. For the few times everything clicks into place – as with using garage doors as panelling in the bathroom here – it seems worth all the dead ends. Reclamation yards are some of my favourite places. My last indulgence or vice is junking; it has all the qualities of a game, a puzzle. What might fit where and what possibilities lie within. The unlocking of houses, and gardens and objects – it is all about making things work for our plot, and it seems we are very much not alone in this occupation.

* * *

There is something elemental in the placing of objects in a landscape. Not elementary, dear reader, but very difficult. We both have an aversion to sculpture gardens, sculpture parks, and sculpture in outdoor places in general. But it can work and when it does it is miraculous and can be heart-breakingly beautiful. As it is with Andy Goldsworthy and Peter Randall-Page, and the perhaps-corporatized-by-fame yet undeniable beauty of Henry Moore in the landscape. And naturally we cannot resist the cheap tricks such as the odd urn or giant capital among ferns. The point is to have fun. Enjoy yourself like Roy Strong. We don't all have to be 'artists'. Shadows and shade seem to work with objects and statues – which are not really our thing; something about a bit of mossy stone in dappled light can be very pleasing. A seat is a good idea, although we are not mad about stone seats: they're too cold for sitting. We like an enclosure: the silver pear at Sissinghurst coupled with its statue, verticality, shape, a story suggested. Often there is a story – this came from a bank in Edinburgh, that carving was a thank-you for something rendered. The point about *objets trouvés,* inside or out, is that they mean something to you.

6
Heavy Water

I f we were to have to move again, God forbid, we both agree that we would go in search of water. The lure of water – the river, the sea, streams to dam and millponds to swim in – is still on the wanted list. Mills, fishing shacks, lifeguard's lookouts, anything with water on Rightmove engenders a terrible disloyalty to Crashington. But for all its faults it does have the pond, fringed with flag iris, dancing with damselflies, dragonflies, mallards and moorhens. The life that water brings is the compelling thing. Since I was tiny, I have loved frogs and toads, newts and snakes. I have quite a number of warty creatures in ceramic form which my family took to giving me from foreign and junking trips. I once lost *the* Bannerman heirloom, a gold watch and chain which, along with its owner, Chelsea Bannerman, survived the Peninsular War and Waterloo only for him to return to Sutherland and bore everyone rigid with bellicose reminiscences. I found the treasure after about seven years of looking – including a thorough search when we moved house. I found it wrapped in a piece of chamois leather and stuffed into the mouth of a Chinese majolica frog.

South Somerset is the land of ditches, or used to be. Every hedge had a ditch, and a more perfect world for invertebrates and birds, surrounded by fly-flicking dairy herds, is hard to imagine. We at least have the organic dairy herd, but so many of the ditches were infilled and that has created so much havoc on the lanes. The ditches and dykes channel the water into the streams and thence to the rivers Isle, Brue, Cam, Cary, Fivehead, Pitt, Parrett and Yeo. Our river is the Yeo, a lazy tributary of the Parrett which it joins at Langport, flowing out from thence into Bridgewater Bay. The father of Andrew Masters, the master builder here, sailed down the Yeo and Parrett on a straw raft all the way to Steart Point. Here, at its midpoint, the river Yeo slumbers along, sunk in deep nettle-clad banks. It took me two years to find a swimming spot, and then everyone said the water will be full of effluent. I do dainty swimming, head-above-water. Mr B feels no such compulsion although his childhood memories are much more water-filled, endless dam building and sparkly swimming in northern tarns and the river Wear. With his strong sense of geography and archaeology he feels very strongly that if you introduce 'fake' water into a garden, you need to be very careful. He is very strict about the likelihood and the context. He hates a pond that has been plonked, whereas I tend to think: well, it's good for wildlife. For Mr B, even a trough must feel like it is spring fed, has come from somewhere and is going somewhere. He likes to make them overflow into a gulley in the floor in the way spring-fed old horse troughs on the edges of villages and towns always did. Mr B is big on limestone troughs, mostly French, but also from these isles in local stones and hence differing colours, depending. They are all things of beauty, timeless and chic. They seem to work anywhere. However, even if the water is just being recirculated, you don't ideally want to realise that. Flat water to mirror the sky and bring it down to the ground, as in East Anglia or here on the Levels, is wonderful. A moat is my dream. Something like a moat or perhaps more an exaggerated ditch is an idea I am always playing with here – but for all its flatness it is difficult to do in a natural and likely fashion. The pond will be great when it has been a bit more bedded in with willow and poplar and I intend to make it swimmable in. This does not interest Mr B in the least – it will come later.

We both have difficulties with the conventional water garden. We both love gunnera, and *Primula florindae* and kingcups, but water is so powerful and simple a thing that the decoration of it with drumstick primulas in dolly-mixture colours somehow grates. Most pleasing are large swathes *or* dainty colonies; I love Californian or Moroccan water courses choked with *Zantedeschia aethiopica* arum lilies. My favourite bit of Geoffrey Jellicoe's garden for Shute House was the use of arum lilies in the simple long tank of water which ended in a Kentian tripartite arch sprinkled with *Wisteria sinsensis*. Lysichiton, the skunk cabbage, has settled like flotsam at one end of the water at the garden we designed at Woolbeding, and from it we took our cue to paint the bridge just that Chinese or skunk-cabbage shade of yellow. There should be enough of just one thing, be it bulrushes, rheums or water lilies. There is so much to choose from it is really hard not to 'go shopping', as we beg our clients not to do. If you think of the wonder of Giverny – and Monet was a man who could shop – in the water garden, at least, it is based on three things: a green bridge, wisteria, waterlilies. No need for drumstick primulas or anything else. It is the same with bulb planting, though here we have fallen fatally into the wanting-too-much trap.

Fountains are not really our thing, well not those kinds of jets you get in public parks at least. We might possibly put a round pool in the centre of the Knights of Yew, because we have a piece of sculpture, a 'water feature', that would work there. But water is such a hassle, so determined to go wrong, so thoroughly devious, so mysteriously strong-willed. If it can get away, run out into the earth, nurture a bed of blanket weed, it will; and if you add in mechanical pumps and I know not what, they will break down and clog up upon the instant. Water is a nightmare in jobs. We always hand over to a specialist as soon as possible. 'Handle with care', says Mr B, but rills we made at Arundel and Woolbeding have worked out beautifully. We can manage a trough with a gurgle, and we think we are quite good at designing desirable pools in which to swim. My all-time favourite fountain, though, is at Stanway in west Gloucestershire. If you want a heart-soaring experience, go in July or August but check it out because it only happens, I think, twice a day and for a limited period of time because it is gravity-fed from a retired reservoir 580 feet above it. No pumps but a lot of pipes and a bit of Torricelli's law and the jet of water rises 300 feet. The jet is in the middle of what was a derelict seventeenth-century water tank or canal, part of the original formal garden of the house. Be there for the initial turn on because it is like a high-pressure rocket; the pent-up energy within is tangible and contagious. The force reverberates through air like a shock wave and reaches max headroom after a couple of minutes, forming a spume and then a nimbus of droplets dancing with prismatic light more than 300 feet above you. Like making the weather. At least this is how it felt on a stultifying July day some years ago, and Mr B has never forgotten it either. For once 'orgasmic' is not an overstatement.

But water in the garden can be welcome as just a flicker of caught light or sound. More water for wildlife is desirable in any garden, even just a bird bath or trough. For most of us, the delight of finding frogspawn is enchantment enough. The ditches round here are clogged with it, even though they are not kept as they were in the old days; this may have a lot to do with the flooding. I would love to make another pond in the back field, but first we need to restore the farmyard pond at the front, and it is a mystery how that and our neighbour's ponds hold water so well as the substrate here is a flint gravel under the loam which drains remarkably freely. Puddled clay at the bottom one imagines – which will make dredging a very delicate operation. Water and turf we leave to the experts. But water is the most fun, the most life-enhancing of all the garden elements. Even swimming pools: they don't have to look like Slim Aarons photos any more.

Mr B and I fundamentally disagree about the fashion for wild swimming ponds. While I sigh over the genius of a house built on a natural swimming pond on *Grand Designs*, Mr B makes French pooffing noises and shrugs. At the garden we designed at Asthall, the conventional pool we put in twenty years ago has been modified by long thin filtration beds either side, making it much prettier and more ecological by far. The steps are a little bit slimy under foot, but Rosie – the owner – and I don't care. Even conventional pools have changed for the better so much that they are almost all a thing of beauty. When pools were just beginning to appear in middle-class gardens in the 1960s, we badgered my father endlessly for one. He could not afford it, he rightly protested, and he so hated the way they were just plonked in walled gardens and orchards with an arrogance and destructive force that pained him. His own sister had a brilliant above-ground pool, made by her husband, repurposing the walls of the old ballroom which had been knocked down to save money at the end of the war. The walls were left about five feet high on three sides with a fourth wall much higher on the gable end where the ballroom had been attached to the rest of the house. From high up here the pool water returned from the rudimentary filter – unheated, of course – into the pool below, via a reconstituted cast of a Renaissance mask, which gave the whole thing an ornamental flavour. I don't think an engineer was consulted; it was simply tanked with cement and painted white, just like an Iberian water cistern or reservoir. This pool was absolutely part of family life in the 1960s, along with the Sodastream and bonfire parties. Mr B had a Catalan girlfriend whose family bathed in a Roman cistern carved from the rock. These are the pools we dream of. Water in Britain is entirely different, cooling and irrigation being less pivotal. We might adore the water tanks by Barragan, but here they would be mostly mossy. Which has its own beauty.

Pools are great, although we need to reconsider how to make them acceptable and avoid the extravagance of heating them with oil. When we built one on the island of Mustique, we heated the water (it seems odd that you should need to, but it was windy and evaporation hugely reduces the temperature of water) by putting pipes under the hot paving around the pool, thereby cooling the paving so that you could walk barefoot on it and warming the water. The important thing is that the pool should be part of the whole composition. Here we are thinking of a 'tank' of water which would look like an Edwardian Jacobean-style garden element. Who knows if it will ever get built. Planning has finally come through after the conservation officer backed down on his conviction that an amorphous shaped pool would be more in keeping with the Elizabethan house. (What 'amorphous' shape exactly did he have in mind – kidney or guitar?) We posted back a pile of rectangular tanks from Tintinhull to Hadspen, Garsington and Hestercombe, and got the permission. Short on money to actually build it, we are long on advice. Plastic liners are actually very good, and now come in dark greys and midnight blues and greens which look great. Automatic covers save money, and the planet, but are expensive. Solar thermal heating is good for the high summer months and air source heat pumps are impressively neat, easy to install and effective, as pool water doesn't need to be that hot, but they still use lots of electricity.

* * *

If you have a pool, you probably have some kind of a pool house. I like a simple 'shanty', as my Irish grandmother called it, a lean-to, half-open and pretty basic. I cannot see the point of a whole Bicester Village of a building with gyms and kitchens and spas and what have you. But that is not my kind of life. If, as I always advocate, a swimming pool in a garden is near enough the house for it not to be a great schlep to get there, then there is no need for an entire satellite station to service it either. If it is near the house, you have all the things you need; while here, Mr B is always on hand with the John Deere Gator (bought thirty years ago after a previous life at the Longleat Center Parc) if we picnic in the orchard and it's too far to carry everything – especially at the end of some light entertainment. If you have a shack, it might be good to have a simple fireplace or, as Logical Child desires, a wood-fired pizza oven. Logical Child is a good cook and a very good pizza maker. His approach is scientific, and he produces from his knapsack an electronic oven thermometer which tells him precisely when the oven has reached the right temperature. Logical Child is also an engineer, so his lockdown escapade was to build a temporary pizza oven in the orchard – a huge success. Together we trawled our home-grown reclamation yard and gleaned a chimney pot; a cast-iron drain cover for the lid, I mean roof; concrete slabs for the floor of the oven; bricks and then mud and straw for the adobe finish. This adobe part meant that the whole thing melted over the following winter, but the principle is set and if we build the shanty the pizza oven will be part of it. It may even come before it. Negotiations are ongoing with Mr B over the exact spot. Wherever it is it will be a warm gravity point for hanging around on long summer evenings, and Logical Child and I have all sorts of cranky ideas to hook up a back boiler inside it and make a makeshift hot tub. More disapproval and raised eyebrows from Mr B.

The point about all this is to enjoy those half-dozen nights of gladness when the stars are out but the dew is heavy in August, and even Russell Page saw the point of an outdoor fireplace, I was chuffed to note. He describes a particular corner for lunching and dining in all weathers – a veranda, I hazard, or covered arbour – for talking and reading and snoozing also, the charm of which was hugely enhanced by the large open fireplace built into the wall 'with only the lilies for fragrance'. We all recognise the elegant luxury of such a scene and equally sitting out under the stars, the braziers burning one's toes. Mr B is the doyen of the brazier. I think he had made some rudimentary ones, and bonfires too, at the alternative midsummer party beside the Firth of Forth when I met him properly for the first time. Always a bit of a pyro like myself and Historical Son, who would like his body to be floated out on a burning longship; Mr B designed and has had made for many clients and friends a round basket on three legs, inspired by those seen in Laurence Olivier's wartime *Henry V*, which is magnificent. Sadly, one client chose to use his pair as urns and filled them with flowers like a hanging basket – but never mind. Horses for courses. Because the cinematic version is rather pricey, Mr B devised a low-grade brazier by attacking a galvanised dustbin with an axe to maximise air flow. He then set the burning bucket on three bricks: picket-line chic. It works a treat, miraculously hotter and more efficient than Henry V's.

7

Husbandry & Wifery

I found myself apologising to a journalist the other evening for the lack of charm and utilitarian nature of the kitchen garden we have made behind Colourful Cottage. Mr B would have berated me: never explain or apologise, everything you do is for a well-thought-out reason. I know he is right about this. The kitchen garden is in a very good place, connected with the main garden and integral to the cottage. It is where rows of cabbages and potatoes were grown in a desultory fashion as shown in the early photos, with willow fencing protection all round – a measure of how even more treeless the farm probably was in former times. We clearly needed some instant shelter also, knowing it would be forever until we built walls. Mr B argued for instant yew hedging, east and west, with the cottage to the south and the poly-folly and overgrown plum hedge to the north. We agreed to make the paths big enough to get a wagon down in anticipation of building things in the section of garden, the hot garden, behind the potting shed and Benton End. As mentioned before, this may become a true walled garden; may have a swimming tank; may have a glasshouse; may have a shanty and a fireplace with a home-made pizza-oven arrangement. But the kitchen garden was to be totally utilitarian: polytunnel, fruit and brassica cages, no-dig beds, wide paths. It lacks charm and consequently is a bit of downer. We will have to work on this. The dahlias will perform, though they take so long to get going, and the nasturtiums can go all over the paths as there is nothing to strangle. But even in September it doesn't look lush enough. It will be sorted. Somehow. Sometime. The poly-folly tunnel has an architectural and utilitarian cool that is what it is. But the Harrod Horticultural fruit cages, which were partly put there to hide the folly tunnel, do not have any cool at all. I wish we had made our own fruit cages in oak as we did at Hanham Court. These were cubes delineated in oak but braced with an X of steel on each side so they looked like a *Flintstones*' version of the Norman Foster Spectrum Building in Swindon. I loved them. But being in a hurry all the time these days we agreed that the black metal mail-order ones would be fine for hiding the poly-folly from our bedroom. The result is the proverbial telly in a Queen Anne cabinet. The telly so much better than the thing to hide it. The kitchen garden is meant to be practical, though; the fruit zoo is fine, but the cruciform path is just too big. Nasturtiums, nasturtiums, we need nasturtiums to spill over. And more arches. However, Mr B says that I am absurdly critical of everything we do, and the point is the husbandry. The raspberries, currants, broad beans and salads are all in, with a lot of help from Connie, who works with us; courgette flowers will come soon, and the sweet peas will swoon. We have to enjoy it.

When Mr B looks at a house, he looks for two things. Where he would put up the Christmas tree, and where he would put a greenhouse. At Ashington neither was obvious. We have now recreated the great hall for the Christmas tree, but not yet the walled garden for the glasshouse. We have the poly-folly, and may never need a glass greenhouse. At Trematon, the Christmas tree dominated the drawing room as it had the high ceiling, and the greenhouse was small and falling apart. For this reason I seemed to gain possession of the greenhouse without anyone noticing. Mr B, 'manfully' as my mother used to say, glued it together with a knitting pattern of nails and two-part car-body filler. He also painted it as often as he could to keep the wet out of the cheap wood. But we never managed to get me in the bucket of a digger to paint the ridge and cresting and top vents. The top vents worked well on those simple, but brilliant, gas-filled pistons. I do like a simple, well-engineered solution to things. I hate the way everything in our lives would now not work if there was a power cut. No landlines? It's so dumb. This greenhouse was about 10 feet by 6 feet (3 metres by 1.8 metres) and had the most awful louvred side windows which were not only harder to open and shut than you could believe possible but the glass slipped out and shattered all the time. Yet, by starting my sweet pea seedlings in propagators in February I staked my claim in the greenhouses, and generally became a rather second-rate tomato-maid in the summer.

In March 2020 we had no greenhouse so we ordered some clear plastic cupboards online. They were fantastic for seedlings and then tomatoes – that is, until they blew away in a storm. Being cheap and plastic, they never were the same again. Tomato growing is all about growing the right ones from seed. Germination is easy, but I still don't really know which are the best to grow. I love 'Gardener's Delight', 'Sungold', 'Micro Cherry' and 'Honeycomb' – any small red cherry tomato. I want a sweet but tangy tomato. If you don't have glass, a hot wall is very productive in a good summer. My big recent discovery is how well basil will do in a cloche. My, how it loves the dry heat. It grows best, I find, in real soil for real flavour and, with a cloche over it, those Neapolitan sulks go away. It never outgrows the cloche because we are always eating it. You can even put a cloche over a pot with basil in it. Simple successes are the best.

All my plants like to listen to Radio 3. They thrive on a balance of music and chat and especially Sean Rafferty. I am not going to begin to give much advice on the lore of the glasshouse as, like vegetable growing, it is not remotely my forte. I know a few things from bitter experience and these I am happy to pass on to anyone. These are: 'Ventilation, ventilation, ventilation.'

Obviously, in winter you want to keep the cold air out, but in summer you cannot get enough air. There comes a moment around Easter when you can and should leave the glasshouse open all day unless it's blowing a Siberian gale. It is imperative to remember to shut it at night, but slightly less disastrous if you have seedlings and cuttings in the inner greenhouse that is the propagator. I have found the propagator invaluable. We use propagators as a greenhouse within a greenhouse. We bought our first propagator on impulse, but it quickly became clear that this would stop the mice from eating my sweet pea seeds before and while they were germinating. The propagator is a box you can seal with a lid, and of course it is warm and toasty so encourages germination or rooting of cuttings. This reduces the likelihood of that other bane, 'damping off' – such an apt description of a situation, relationship or professional arrangement when it goes all mouldy. Many slightly more sophisticated greenhouses have a warmer section, sometimes a 'mist house' or inner plastic arrangement – a sort of mini jungle. I have about seven propagators. Because they speed things up, I can move stuff out of them once the aforementioned dangers are past and start all over again with tomatoes or whatever. Keep your greenhouse simple. Everyone could use unlimited bench space for growing, for propagators, for potting up, for the radio. Also a broom and dustpan. The hose arrangements are important – it is worth investing in a really good lance for shower-like watering. In the poly-folly the pelargoniums have to jostle with the seedlings until they are allowed out at night, at which point they are superseded at about the same moment by the tomatoes. I used to grow tomatoes in pots because it seemed easier and looks a lot prettier; however, in the poly-folly they can grow in the ground, which is fantastic. We grew them with basil and tagetes, strong and smelly, as companions last to keep the whitefly at bay.

Here at Ashington, Mr B is king of the greenhouse. We might have a glasshouse one day but for now we are thrilled – well, he is particularly thrilled – with the poly-folly, the Keder Greenhouse. Made of bubble-wrap-like plastic and an aluminium frame, it was a good buy; designed and built in Germany, they are supplied by a firm in Evesham. There was no divergence in opinion about getting a Keder. Our neighbour in Cornwall had had one for over twenty years. There was discussion and divergence as to where it was to go. It's not bad looking, quite modern and cool in fact, if a bit plastic. The sides are covered with green net so less of the offensive bubble shows. I cannot remember my preferred slot and, as with so many things in life, after all the agonising and debate it seems like no other solution would have worked. Further east was my feeling, now I think about it; more out of the way. But Mr B said he wanted to have it quite handy as it is pivotal in his daily deliberations round the garden – and he was right, of course. It is in the currently rather unsatisfactory kitchen garden.

When I first met Mr B, he knew so much more about everything than I did about anything (I could barely tell an oak from a beech). Like Walter, his will naturally prevailed. But Walter only gardened with Margery for less than ten years. How things change. I was always a little know-all, of course, and thoroughly opinionated in my heart. I was just unused to voicing opposition, being the youngest of five. Unfortunately or otherwise, I have become infinitely more confident thanks to Mr B. He schooled me in speaking out. Told me to say boo to many geese. As a result, I am now Bossyboots, the Führer and other monikers denoting the much less charming and sweet, the vociferous and sometimes angry me of middle age. But Mr B is always generous, even when proved wrong, and he remembers and remains so. I remember nothing, which is quite a blessing I believe. And when he kindly says, for instance, 'You were right about the *Cercis* going there,' I am shocked to discover I had any hand in it at all.

The Keder is his fiefdom. Tall enough to take his daturas (brugmansias as they now are), this is the first winter he has kept them alive above ground. In fact, he kept them in flower by leaving an electric fan on. By some miracle the new 'smart meter' ceased to operate almost the moment it was put in. The bill has been estimated, but on pre-Christmas usage. But, delightful as it was to step into a Moroccan courtyard in February, if he wants a heated Keder we will need to put in a small ground source system, or so Logical Child suggests. However, being made of bubble wrap the Keder is frost free. I check the overnight thermometer most mornings with the pug and we are both in a sort of trance of amazement. And from the ventilation-in-summer point of view, it is as intelligently practical as its German origins would suggest. The problem of top ventilation – which in a glasshouse or a groovy atrium is absolutely essential to creating air flow – is solved by the top of the walls of the Keder opening up to let out the heat, thereby sucking in fresh cool air at floor level. Most of both sides are on a thermostatically controlled roller and roll down from the top like magic, just as far as they think fit. This automation is fantastic, as the tomato-maid will be inside ventilating her computer, and mostly useless in the garden. Not only useless but inconsistent. Which is the worst way to garden. I rush out and interfere. Cut things back, sow seeds madly, pick loads and dream up new ideas. Then I find two weeks has flown by, we were away that weekend, got Covid, forgot everything because of Covid, and I have done nothing; everything has turned to ashes.

Gardening is so plodding and consistent. That is why it is such a Buddhist and calming protocol for life. Like animals and children, it requires a continence and reliability very absent in modern life. I really admire the discipline of true gardeners: allotment holders who get down there – sometimes a long way from home – regularly, and keep things just so. Watering, bug spotting, weeding all require a military approach. Mr B has to be the husband, though. He is the good shepherd. He nannies his plants through and truly cares. He thinks I am an absentee landlord. My brain is too absent. Thank God he's there or there would be no garden to boast about. My forte is weeding, because it is almost always necessary, and I can give it half an hour or four hours and do good. I hate the thugs. I could weed for England in the Olympics. It has the benefit for me of being something you can pick up and put down; if you get called away to the phone you might carry on two days later. It can be done without consultation or confrontation but with immense gratification. I love weeding. It is mindful without being aimless. It gets results and is essential. I don't even really find it boring.

Irises 'Strathmore', 'Sable', and 'Jane Phillips' with love-in-a-mist, roses, peonies, 'Tequila Flame' lupins and, in the background, wisteria and green oak pillars, May 2022.

The bellcote, with the Knights of Yew
beehives and iris planting, May 2022.

Above: Benton End through
the iris beds, 2022.

Right: the tool shed with *Rosa*
'The Garland', lavender and sweet
Williams, 2022.

Left. By the west terrace:
Rosa 'Madame Isaac Péreire',
with brugmansia on the
right and *Matthiola incana*
'Pillow Talk' in front, 2022.

Above: towards the studio door: 'Gladiator'
lupins, sweet Williams, Hidcote lavender, *Geum*
'Totally Tangerine' and *Rosa* 'Gypsy Boy', 2022.

Overleaf: The front drive in June 2022.

I like doing it any time, with or without listening to a book on Audible (which is, of course, the greatest breakthrough in my lifetime). Only my wrists are letting me down. So it has to be in short spells – which is perfect.

The pleasure that even a small greenhouse can bring is the way it extends the season. It gives one a place to go and nurture things like plumbago, jasmine, even earlier paperwhite narcissi and Roman hyacinths – or auriculas, which I love, but I don't seem to have the touch for them. One doesn't have to grow anything difficult or clever to get pleasure out of it. Scale can be an issue for constructions. You need to sort of pick a height for everything: fruit cage, Keder, polytunnel, greenhouse, apple or rose arches. These need to fit the proportions of the space, and the proportions want to look handsome and not mean. Once you have this set – and this is where 3D drawing applications like 'Sketchup' can help (although they give quite an odd visualisation, whereas with practice your brain is so much better at imagining these things) – you should have good parameters fixed. Mr B might differ. But for him big is always better. However, in the kitchen garden here the Keder, which is about eight feet tall, arrived first and set the scale. Our fruit cage is not the best looking. Like the rose arches. But it is good value. My plan is to paint all of these rather plasticky-looking black constructions with a paint which claims to make everything look like corten steel – ready rusted. Now this would be a breakthrough; but I am not sure if Mr B will agree, and Emotional Child said it was a terrible idea, rather to my surprise.

* * *

I am also waiting for the compost bins to arrive, to get built that is, as promised for my last several birthdays. There is always something more pressing than my compost bins in construction-land where I live. Mr B and I have always been big on mulch, though, buying 'Rejuvenate Compost' (as Sherborne Turf call their council compost), but finding the time to make compost has just not happened. Until recently I always thought compost was for *pedants*, but I am learning now that the *pedosphere* is the scientific classification of the soil layer of the Earth, companion to the more familiar atmosphere. Of course, this is the medium for plant growth, water storage, the atmospheric regulator extraordinaire, the great carbon sink; and yet we just dig it up and dump it full of waste and trash it with poisons. An oil man once 'explained' to me how *unimportant* the Earth's crust is because if you were to look at a section through the Earth, and think of it like time measured by a clock, it is only the last few seconds of the story, just as we are in history. So it's nothing, was his argument; nothing if we frack it and crack it. But that is exactly the point: it is so fragile, like the atmosphere; we destroy it at our peril. He didn't get it. Compost convert that I now am, I intend to join the compost-makers in a big way in this new garden – *when* I get good bins in which to make compost. It may slip down the list of priorities with monotonous regularity, but it will happen, and how good it will be for the soil.

It's almost a spiritual experience, running soil through your hands, kneading the clod to feel its make-up and propensities, how it sticks together or to your fingers, smeary or granular, scrunching into a stable ball or crumbling away. When we are in a new garden it is never long before, like Mole in *The Wind in the Willows*, Mr B plugs in his paws, catching the telegraphic signals from down below. He looks for molehills, those unfairly despised heaps of delicious friable loam on your lawn. Moles are the megafauna of the underworld, and moles mean worms, because they mine those galleries on the hunt for worms, and worms are much more abundant in a healthy open loam. Respect the mole and live with his hills, for he represents the good health of your underworld. Earthworms understandably eschew extremes and like to hang around most in neutral soils of around pH 7–7.5 (the thing with pH – the measure of the acidity or alkalinity of the soil – is that it is a logarithmic scale, so half a point is a massive difference in sweet or sourness). The more extreme your terroir, acidic or alkaline, the fewer the worms and the more specific the underground fauna and the fungi, which are generally acid tolerant. Most normal garden soils need to be opened and lightened up, and we all know that organic matter is the key magic soil improver. I remember now with shame how in the 1980s we would buy bales of sphagnum moss peat – an acidifier from all that carbon it captures, and fast running out – to sweeten and lighten our garden soil. Now bio-char is the thing, a fantastically stable charcoal.

The bounty of vegetables we grew this first year here, in that 2020 war-footing, land-girl, landlocked, lockdown strangeness, was miraculously without pests and diseases. No blackfly on the beans. This is how we need to keep it. Our experience this first season seems to confirm that garden tools break up existing structure in undisturbed soil (ours had been left untilled for thirty years), the structure which maintains and develops a honeycomb of small air passages. Many or most of these have been made by either worm movement (fantastically slow, which is why they get massacred by machine tools) or generations of hyphae – tiny threads put out by mycorrhizal fungi, which push microscopic boreholes through the soil and then die, leaving only air or water. While alive, they symbiotically provide the biological link between root and soil, taking sugars down from plants and water and mineral nutrients such as phosphates up to the plants.

What else can we do? We can leave the leaves, or at least collect them in a pit in the garden where they will make crumbly brown mulch with immodest haste. Three times last November perfectly sane people said to me how dispiriting it is to rake up leaves from their lawns each day only to have more fall in the night – somehow implying the spitefulness of trees. 'Why bother though?' I beg of them. 'What does it matter if your lawn looks a bit of a mess?' Why not instead watch the miracle take place? Have you ever seen how leaves stick up like the shark's fin in *Jaws* in the morning, pulled down into the subterranean nightclub by so many wriggly hermaphrodites? Feeding the soil, aerating the lawn without your having to lift a finger or a rake, let alone a leaf blower.

Of course, the truth is that to make our own compost we would need Mr B on board and doing all the work a lot of the time, as he does with the watering. Mr B does watering like a vocation. It is a skill. It is an act that requires concentration: you need to be thinking and actively engaged, not messing about, mind elsewhere. You need to be working out which plant needs what. Particularly if you are watering plants in pots in trays. It is so easy to completely miss some, and you need to have the hose right down at soil level in each pot. I don't really trust even the good shower attachments, although they are excellent for some things, and their gentleness in not moving the soil about can be essential. That's another thing about watering: the amateur makes holes in the soil or flushes the compost out of the pot. It is skilled labour. Mr B always says he is exhausted after watering, because like any task worth doing well it means concentrating. Other surprising garden skills that require commitment are raking and hoeing. Where I learnt to dig and delve I don't really know but I think it was from watching first my brother and then Mr B. I was acting out a part at first. Slowly you become the part and you learn the art. It is important not to do yourself an injury while doing repetitive jobs like this. You need to use your core and stand solidly, slightly soft knees and straight back. Pilates has saved me; without it I would be crippled by my arthritis and forty years of wear and tear. Mr B does nothing to save himself but then he is a machine. The parts and bearings are wearing a bit thin. He has the new half knee. But he is still, incredibly, undaunted and made of titanium. However, we should have been more sensible. We should have listened to his mother: she always warned us.

8
Plantwifery

When Mr B and I started gardening together four decades ago, there were garden centres and nurseries, but it was still the case that if you wanted to order unusual things – hellebores from Helen Ballard behind the Malvern Hills, say – you posted a stamped addressed envelope for her to send you her list. Then you sent a cheque in the post with your list taken from her list. Then you might go there to pick up the 'slips' – slithers of plant material cut through the root – or they would appear in the post many months later, wrapped in damp newspaper. Why has everything got so much more elaborate? Times were greener, even in the 1980s. Before the explosion of the garden centre, everyone took and gave away cuttings. Much was posted, or pilgrimage was made to visit a specialist grower. Their names are a sort of almanac of professionalism: John Massey, Elizabeth Strangman, Graham Gough – who is still producing wonderful plants – and many others. Visiting a grower is still one of the great pleasures of gardening, although we don't get to do it as much as we should or would like to. When hellebores were our passion, we had to work hard to visit Helen Ballard, and we had the best time with Will McLewen at his place in Manchester. One wintry afternoon we drove to Stockport, and he was there between plant-collecting trips to Bosnia during the war there. There is attraction about the obsessive which always gets me, but you need to know just enough to keep them interested. Visiting Helen Ballard we would make a slow royal progress round the garden, her in her disability carriage carrying a long bamboo stick which she used to lift the flower heads in order to see what they looked like inside. It was a treat and an education. Mr B was very good with her and she slowly melted into generosity mode and pressed more slices upon us than we had remotely paid for. She had a team of two who were sent off to fetch a sharp spade. She then began to make them slice off pieces of choice plants, not usually for sale, such as 'Greencups' – a particularly round and globular acid-green hellebore she had bred, with flowers like Granny Smith apples. We gave some of our plants eventually to the garden designer and serious plant aficionado Mary Keen, who gave us some back when she moved house. The generous freemasonry of gardeners has always worked this way.

When we first got to Ashington and opened all the doors and spilled out into the garden there was grass everywhere, with a line of shrubs and a gate in the corner before the south-facing wall which joins into the potting shed. The potting shed is naturally the pivotal point of the garden. And very lucky we are to have it. It forms a natural cross axis, with a pathway running through it, and its low red roof and timbered end have something of the 'gardens of a golden afternoon', a Miss Jekyll-ishness about it. It is the first time we have had a proper tool shed in the middle of our garden. We are both terribly untidy with tools and blame each other all the time for losing them, leaving them out or in the wrong place. Sadly, neither of us possesses that careful, mending and sharpening nature which would be so useful. But, like everything we do, there is method in our madness and it's something we understand between us. The potting shed is currently very open, which was good for the swallows but we think the jackdaws have frightened them off. It might be useful to make it more enclosed someday, but we like the view through and we would love the swallows to return. Meanwhile it is stacked up with outdoor furniture in winter, and in summer it is a good tool shed; mowers and string and the copper tools – which are really good – all live here. Behind it is where the barrows gather, and is more of a messy area. All gardeners need a messy area, it is just the nature of things. I have always been slightly dispirited by the tides of trailer-park trash that some growers survive in, but they are always run off their feet, going to plant fairs, packing up vans while watering, feeding, transplanting, running around like blue-arsed flies. No wonder there is almost an inverse ratio: the better the plant nurturer, the messier the nursery. Some growers are military, but on the whole I would suggest that husbandry attracts people who like a little chaos – animals and plants generally coming before the tidiness of their yards or motors. There was no plastic swamp in my uncle Anthony's market garden. It might have been messy but everything was made of match wood, those charming boxes and trays that you still get Christmas tangerines in, or paper or clay pots. But rapidly this changed and such operations became an impasto abstraction of printed plastic bales and twine, bread crates and towers of plastic pots, fading legends and sun-cracked concrete. The romance has gone. The horticultural trade really needs to get its act together, clean up, be pesticide free, peat free, plastic packaging free – mail order packing is insane – and become more sustainable.

Back to the corner. In the elbow of the extended potting-shed wall, near the broken gate, was a happy patio to which everyone gravitated. The wisteria had been planted here in the Sandemans' time and they had put down enough paving for a table and chairs. It is a great place to go for eggs on toast in the full sun of the morning; for lunch in the shade of the wisteria; and for tea or drinks to look back at the west face of the house fading in the gloaming. We might add a bit more paving, and already we have the big gravel path coming down to it from the studio. We might add a gurgle of water on the wall so that anyone lurking behind cannot hear what is being said. The wall was pregnant with a big bulge when we moved in, and quickly this exploded on to the floor and had to be patched up. The bed that encloses it has the path from the stair tower on the other side. In design terms there are technically too many equal axes going this way. It works well enough, although I think some sort of cross axis to take you from here to the rose garden is probably going to evolve. The area outside the studio was choked with sycamore seedlings, and a decent Irish yew which it was a pity to lose but which was bang in the way of the view through the potting shed and casting too much shade. We have made up for it by planting the twenty-three Yew Knights.

We brought a lot of irises with us from Trematon. In general, my advice on moving house is not to move plants with you. It seems tempting, but it is a nightmare and a huge job to pot them and keep them going. Much better start again with 7- or 9-centimetre plants, I promise you, from experience. The iris, though, are a bit like the hellebore slips: you can dig up the rhizomes and chuck them in a box and then chop them up and plant them when you get to the other end. They can take a bit of neglect, and being small they handle well and can be planted quickly. This meant we had to agree where to plant them quickly. Luckily this was a decision that made itself: under the hot south-facing wall, where there had been a border and the soil is rich but free draining. Then we added the path all the way from the studio/cider room door (the door came about a year later but we knew it was going to be there). This copycat axis would have irises both sides, the wide path would have pinks and erigeron in the gravel, and the background a medley of cottage-garden flowers: roses, hollyhocks, sweet Williams, lupins, columbines, peonies, snapdragons, some delphiniums crept in, orange geums, and the odd fennel and artichoke. In 2020 this was chives, carrots, kale, rocket, shallots, and all kinds of things, with the tomato cupboards and green beans along the back wall. A chaos of pigeon netting and courgettes – it was great. Much happier than the proper boot camp for vegetables which we got going last year. But that will come right with some thought.

I always have this regret for the first few seasons of a new garden, when the 'sacrificial planting' is more enchanting than all that you carefully planned out on paper. In order to assuage the impatient client, or indeed our own impatience, we always add in sacrificial planting to make up for the roses being small in the beginning, and shrubs too, all the 'body' plants – philadelphus, daphne, artichokes or *Crambe cordifolia,* for instance. They are all so much diminished in comparison to their planned presence in the scheme that we cannot resist throwing in anchusa, tobacco plants, antirrhinums, love-in-a-mist, poppies, all the scatterable or sow-straight-in-the-ground fun things like zinnias. These prototype beds are more relaxed and dancing than anything you could plan on paper. If only one could keep it like this. The second year is usually the best, when the big things are beginning to be established, but here we are in our fourth summer. This seems so grown up, and it is looking grown up. A friend said to me that it is working now as the design intended; that you can feel the overall structure quite clearly in all the different parts, with their individual moods, but their contribution to the whole remaining apparent. At Hanham Court there was anchusa everywhere for the first two years, with larkspur, the annual delphinium: spires of blue much better than any thought-out scheme. Ashington flushed the second year with a million opium poppies. Such a dream for two or three weeks. It is very hard to modulate a garden to make it work like this. Chelsea chopping – cutting back in May – is very useful as things get established and sometimes too big too early. Also, I am experimenting with the idea of chopping back the fennel in May. I haven't actually managed it, but it would be good because it is the low frondy pondy growth at the same level as the herbaceous that we like so much, although we do also like the taller, thinner effect of it when in acid-coloured flower. The search for high wands is partly what all the grasses enthusiasm is about. I only like the oaty grasses (and then only the ones which don't have too much of wig factor going on at the bottom). I love thalictrums for this wandy quality and they seem to be quite easy to grow but not to keep for long. Patrinia does this job brilliantly but we have had little luck with growing it. Umbellifers like dill, parsnip, ridolfia and selinum all do it with varying degrees of success. Sweet clover is good but in experimental mode only for us, so far. There is a loose, windy perfection that we are all striving for, but this is only one goal of many, and our gardening life is about making us happy. It is not a competition.

In March 2020 Mr B raced over to a small grower near Wells and bought all their Benton irises, and we filled out our own one-year-old iris borders – which were all *Iris pallida*, 'Jane Phillips', 'Sable' and 'Braithwaite' – with a palette of fleshy pinks and browns, bruised purples and blues, various veined beauties with golden beards and enormous Georgia O'Keefe falls. Cedric Morris bred flowers at Benton End for the painting thereof; they are amazing but almost obscene. I prefer the ginger, cinnamon, toffee and mahogany-coloured ones we ordered from Woottens of Wenhasten and Iris Cayeux. Here at Ashington we do not usually indulge in painstaking colour-palette analysis, but with the Hamstone and the gravel it does make some sense to pick up upon the gingery brown notes, to mix warmth with cool blues. In the end we mix everything with everything. It's all a bit like dahlias: if you have enough colours thrown in together you get a sweet shop, and that has its own beauty and vibrance. Monocultures are dangerous and the irises do need a lot of careful husbandry after flowering. Last year Helen, who works with us, suggested the sowing of love-in-a-mist along with the iris. Not really expecting them to germinate, I scattered seed rather too liberally. The result has been electrifying. The intensity of the blobs of colour from the iris is somehow melded and welded by the bright blue and fairy fringes of the nigella. The results are way beyond all our expectations. Well done, Helen, says Mr B. But we are all a bit anxious about the smothering factor. As soon as the irises are over, I suggested, the nigella will have to be brutally thinned in an agonising and laborious process which will involve hours on our bottoms pulling out and cutting back. The iris leaves are looking peaky beneath all that fluff, so they clearly need freeing up and ventilating. Mr B says the nigella seed heads look amazing and he doesn't want to see the peaky iris leaves. So be it, say I – but you will rue the day! The nigella will never go away, I suspect, like the nasturtiums. I have to pull the self-sowers out daily. The iris rhizomes need to bake in the sun after flowering, to build up strength for next year. But it must be worth all the work. The three weeks of show-stopping colour and brilliance we have had this year have been worth it.

This garden has an aspect which needs more understanding to be able to work with. It gets little sun in the morning, especially near the house. This is great for things that hate to be warmed too quickly after a night's frost, such as tree peonies and camellias. It is not the country for camellias, but I had high hopes for the tree peonies, though they are taking an age to get going. The studio garden being a small courtyard really, with the high gable of our bedroom to the south, is shady. This was great for growing salads and certain vegetables which bolt in the hot dry sun. Much fruit is also better for shade, currants particularly. The roses we chose to cover this rather ugly wall then were 'Albéric Barbier' and 'Madame Alfred Carrière'. But near the studio the garden has a temporary air as we have permission to make a 'garden room', something single-storied and lightweight, to connect the house with the cottage through the studio. Whether it will ever come to fruition is doubtful, but because of this long-term plan, I somehow thought we were being half-hearted about this bit. But I was completely wrong and Mr B has quietly stuffed it with a globby, luscious mix of delphinium, sweet William and geums, edged with Hidcote lavender and pinks of all sorts. It is pink, crimson, delft blue, orange and deep purple at the moment – like a duvet which begs you to dive in. It is spectacular in a way I suspect it will never be again. Serendipity springs up in any garden quite unexpectedly. The truncated body of an ancient pear tree is hanging on to another bulging wall which we have packed with dry cement and hope to keep together somehow. There is jasmine on the north wall, because it does famously well, being one of those plants which can survive the frost if it does not get warmed over too quickly in the morning. Wallflowers will always be a favourite. I love them best in walls. That's where I planted them first as a small child. Historical Child loves them in the ancient walls of

Canterbury where he works, realising with astonishment how long they must have been self-seeding away there. There is also an ancient colony growing in the flint and lime of the walls of Ely Cathedral Precinct.

At the back of the cider barn, Colourful Cottage is now the studio. But its garden is the kitchen garden to the north and the wonderful kitchen courtyard to the south where we will be looking out from the new scullery of the old manor as we do mountains of washing up. We have not had the heart or the energy to even really discuss this kitchen court and how it will be planted. I know that Mr B would like to use the cobbles he has been collecting. Mr B would like box bushes, and I would like a washing line. We have found an ancient Hamstone surround for the well that's there. Cottagey it will be, but I hope a bit severe. The east-facing façade of the house, the reverse of the west-facing side that is on to the garden, is very strong, with two monumental chimney stacks; Mr B thinks they remind him of a continental two-pin plug. The staircase and cloakroom have an Escher-like catslide of roofs, and the scullery was supposed to look like an estate joiners shop with a lot of windows, only the planners tried their best to make this as mundane as possible. The importance of humble everyday planting to go with vernacular everyday architecture is very close to our hearts. Understatement cannot be overstated. Honesty, periwinkle, ivy, poppies – Welsh or opium – all are welcome here, anywhere here, the more random the better. I admit to being almost perverse in my espousal of un-plantiferous plants. I love the unfashionable, and the long-forgotten: alyssum, stachys and an aquilegia of any kind. I love *Thalictrum flavum* for its salix yellow dusters; elder bushes and buddleia in places are essential on a farm of this kind. The sallows and pussy willows, too, and *Buddleja globosa*, whose golden blobs go with the stone here, as do all the purples and oranges of the buddleia family. Macleaya would be interesting to use and perhaps romneya will romp away as it did much to my surprise at Trematon. I had never got it to work before, but there it was becoming a weed. We have planted onopordums – my favourite thistle, like a Scottish embroidery – in the rose garden, with clouds of gypsophila against the aquamarine of sea kale, with its own, momentary gypsophila-like blooms, and sea holly. And there is the big *Crambe cordifolia* – in the background with the onopordum, phlox, gaura and 'Electric Blue' penstemon. A late flowering shimmering haze, says Mr B, getting all lyrical.

Roses are never far from our thoughts. Only just in this fourth season can we see the roses becoming a thing. 'Gypsy Boy', 'Souvenir du Docteur Jamain' and 'Madame Isaac Péreire' are at last beginning to have a presence with their saturated colour and smell. As stated, we have a compulsion to overplant. At home this is all right. At work it can mean that the thugs take over if not carefully watched during those initial seasons. Mr B never follows a plan; he paints with his pots of plants. It's instinctive: you see the future in your mind's eye – you almost switch off the conscious mind – and though I know I can do this too, I think he is much better at it. This shows when he plants a big pot out; it somehow looks better than anyone else's from the start. Mr B also starts to think in colour only really after he has set out the body of a bed. Usually, on a job, we have drawn up a plan in minute detail so that we can order the plants. But he will not follow the plan. This must be understood. The plan is the palette. When the plants arrive, generally in pots, they are his paint box and he always says: why didn't you get more of this and what I am going to do with all that stuff? First to go in are the shrubs and roses. He suggests planting five little shrubs together, be it Persian lilac, hydrangeas or roses such as 'Blanche Double de Coubert'. Eventually they will form great mounds.

Mr B never picks up his bits either. He is a really good policeman, deadheading like fury and trimming and prinking all the time with his secateurs. Usually under pressure, he tends to let the trimmings fall in the bed. We both flick the finished iris flowers and their instantly swelling ovaries into the far corners of the bed – possibly spreading disease that way. But like Margery Fish, I try to be what she called the 'fifth gardener': an imaginary extra person who trails behind picking up bits and weeding the gravel. It is annoying to bend down and pick up the prickly bits of roses when they could have been collected neatly in a trug or bucket at the time. But I understand that time is of the essence, and it is the deadheading that matters not the rubbish-picking. It is an honourable role, the fifth gardener.

* * *

Colour in planting is a subjective and enormous subject. Green is green and is the most important colour of all. Beyond that we have a love of colour and no particular theories. Mr B went to art school but I work only intuitively. I am an anarchist. Colour is inherently life enhancing, the prism of a jet of water, iridescence, irises. Far too many people, though, are afraid of colour. The white garden at Sissinghurst is about colour and completely beautiful; it has been a design impossible for anyone to spoil. It is an apogee which makes it difficult to follow, an impossible trope. We like to do cool planting, in sideshow areas or upon arrival very often, or a calm anteroom.

The colour people seem to be most afraid of is yellow. Which is curious considering we all love a daffodil, a buttercup, a primrose, a dandelion. Perhaps it is fear of forsythia and kerria and the brassy yellows of just those daffodils I do not enjoy. I am a bit worried by the brassy look of my *Tulipa sylvestris* so liberally scattered down either side of the drive. On their own in a vase they have a shimmering sulphurous yellow of Chinese silk, but en masse, with the snake's-head fritillaries cowed by them, at a distance they look dangerously like great splodges of 'King Alfred' daffodils. It will be difficult to unplant them now. Recently I saw fritillaries accompanied just by cowslips and I nearly cried at the daintiness. The chrome yellow of crown imperial fritillaries seems difficult to place, and the orange ones too. I think they are best in pots as they are so artificial looking. Like eucomis, they look like a painting when in pots. However, I have seen them naturalised under trees and they look astonishing. But yellow really is the colour of spring and immensely welcome. Later in the year, or perhaps if you have a very red brick house, it becomes a problem. But we just ignore clients who say they don't want yellow or white or whatever colour it is they want to proscribe.

It is absurd. They never notice. I mean yellow comes in so many hues and subtleties, from pale and acidic to hot and smouldering.

Our old friend David Vicary loved the 'muds of England', as he called all those colours from drab to willow yellow. Willows in fact abound in variegations of bark colour which are or should be the envy or bible of interior decorators. Subtle but rich are the shades of willow bark, from primrose to almost lacquer red. But bark colour has never been something Mr B and I have felt at home with using as a design trope. I know they are amazing, but we have never succeeded in making a story around coloured bark that works. The Japanese do it, as do urban courtyards; perhaps disconnected spaces can do it. Or perhaps the reverse – loosely, as if by mistake, in a copse you could do it, but a bit of garden which says 'look at my bark' doesn't do it for me, or Mr B. Prejudice corner again.

It is difficult to use yellow roses sometimes. And yet it shouldn't be. Some of my favourite roses are the group of climbers called Noisettes, which were developed in the US in the nineteenth century and provided the first real repeat-flowering climbers to grace our gardens. We used these to fabulous effect at Asthall Manor – where they are beautifully tended and have almost engulfed the house. Since childhood I have loved the rose 'Gloire de Dijon' because it grew in a broken-down greenhouse at East Hendred when I was small and impressionable. I have sadly never managed to grow it well, and possibly, along with my other favourite, the pink 'Souvenir de la Malmaison', it has somehow lost vigour in its breeding. I think this can happen. In any commercial growing, the stock from which plants are propagated can be poor; perhaps it can even become poor. But then, in our rather industrialised systems of production these days, with huge firms producing most stock, if a poor strain gets to be dominant and then gets a reputation for being a weakling it will fall out of favour. When lots of little nurseries and people produced plants from their local breeding stock, perhaps an old rose found on a castle wall, there was more vigour and variety in the genetic material. Hence you can see an amazing example of a rose, say at Mottisfont or Sissinghurst, but what you buy with alacrity and anticipation at your local source will not necessarily be of the same calibre. I will keep trying with 'Gloire de Dijon' and one day hit on a decent strain. One way is to buy from smaller nurseries in different parts of the country whenever you travel about. I like the added dimension to a plant when you can – and this is increasingly rare – remember the day and the place and the happiness with which you bought it. A souvenir of a maison, or a sojourn or a breakdown – mechanical or emotional.

Here at Ashington the walls are digestive-biscuit golden so we feel more confident about yellows – although the really cadmium ones are still difficult to place. In roses I love *Rosa helenae* hybrid – banana cream coloured, and fruitily scented also with a shimmer of bananas. 'Lady Hillingdon' is Angel Delight egg-yolk yellow and she should hold her own with the stone. 'Maigold' and 'Golden Wings' are things we are trying and it's been a long time. We tried them at The Ivy also because David Vicary was a big fan. Oh those stamens, he would say. 'Goldfinch' I have loved since childhood – so Mr B has to put up with it. 'Buff Beauty' was a DV favourite as well – for me, it's a bit too polite, or maybe there is something modern about it which irks me, but there is no question but that it does brilliantly, as do all the other Pemberton repeating roses. 'Nevada' is a primrose yellow and I always envy it in other gardens but somehow have failed to make it really work for me. *R. primula* is a favourite rose of mine, both for its starry fragile flowers and for its scented frondy leaves. I think it is a million times more worthwhile than 'Canary Bird', which everyone grows. But, of course, there is a catch. It is slow to establish and not a great grower once settled in. It is something you have to nurture and hence a bit of a rarity and a special child. Whereas 'Canary Bird' is a doer.

Other yellows not to be missed: the palest yellow of the giant scabious is exactly the 1950s hue that I love. In fact, scabious yellow is a good term for this elusive sulphurous primrose colour that has some green in it and fights with no man.

Mr B and I have a problem with purple leaves. Wordsworth, says Mr B, hated the copper beech, presumably introduced during the eighteenth century and reaching maturity in Wordsworth's time, because it created black holes in the landscape. And, of course, this is true. In a black and white photograph, the tonality of purple is very black, very hole-like. Mirabel Osler says that purple cotinus are very hard to place; the colour of broken veins, they are often left abandoned like a beached summer pudding in the middle of a lawn. We have never and would never plant one. They just don't do it for us on any level.

* * *

I think it is common among gardeners to regress through their gardening life to the simpler things, the more understated, the wilder, the single-flowered species. And I think as we have all become increasingly conscious of the ecological storm which is brewing up, we need to move away from importing specimens in containers of peat-based compost and go back to making cuttings from friends' gardens, locally, and growing from seed. Although we are known as extravagant, romantic and almost theatrical gardeners and designers, Mr B and I have been leaning more this way for twenty years, experimenting with our woodland garden at Hanham Court where the understorey of hazel was host to species rambling roses. In our garden at Trematon Castle, we flung species rambling roses at the walls and tried to blend the borders with a wildling fringe of grass seeded with wild carrot, *Daucus carota,* and wild echium, moon daisies and white camassia. Here in Somerset, we have a cider orchard and very few mature trees in a flat landscape. We are planting 2 acres of woodland which will take some time, so meadow-making is the thing. On top of ox-eye daisies and viper's bugloss and wonderful perennial seed mixes, we have planted plugs of wild flowers and species bulbs which we hope will naturalise. This is not the 'naturalistic' gardening of prairie and perennial meadow so much as old-fashioned wild flowers and natives mixed with cottage-garden familiars and things which suit the climate and soil conditions and do not require cosseting.

The garden here is very conventional. We make no excuses, although the rose garden is so conventional we really need to work something out. One day it will be the aquarium for a huge monster octopus of a rose, for *Rosa* 'Mulliganii' will devour the silly arches and central dome. Far and few are the growers of real old roses, and species old roses even farther. But we want this box simply filled with white foam, maybe a white garden. We have hedged our bets with *R. helenae*, because we love it and we love Helen, who has worked with us for twenty-five years. We made the space last year, drawing with yew hedging and a cruciform path. The beds were weeded and heavily mulched. We mulched over the planting in our minds through the winter. This year the rather cheap and nasty rose arches arrived and got put up by Brian. Mr B is most sceptical about my inclination to paint them so I will have to find the paint and paint them myself, when I get a free weekend. And soon, before the newly planted roses send fishing rods out which will need tying in. The plants have arrived and been planted; 'Memory' pinks, crambe, onopordum, white phlox and some mistaken *Erysimum* 'Bowles's Mauve'. Mostly white, but half-hearted. Tending towards late, I can see some tobaccos filling in, and cosmos. Mr B said no to dahlias. It's still in the experimental phase. Maybe it will come right, or it could be one of those bits which never works. I find this syndrome happens in many things.

But to cheer one up something else goes right. The nut tree garden next door is rocketing away with shuttlecock ferns and more ferns on their way. The winter flowers have melted: there were primroses with scillas, sarcococca and skimmias (not a pleasing plant but a pleasing smell), and before that there were snowdrops and aconites with hellebores. All vanished and forgotten, now that a dappled duvet of fronds has emerged from the brown earth, traced back and forth by the mole. The little paths are blistered with mole runs, making the ground airy and squishy, meaning healthy, beneath the clodden feet. Mr B has always had a friendship and affinity with ferns that I have watched with interest. The old owner of Fibrex fern (and pelargonium) Nurseries showed him how to fill a car with ferns, laying them on their sides, without damaging them. And when Mr B plants them, he does it with an assurance born of an understanding with them. Like horse whisperers, those who handle plants with confidence never hurt them, though they might appear to throw them around with insouciance. Placing them like a painter, their relationship assured and non-combative, the plants then thrive.

I think Mr B visualises very surely, adding unexpected species whose form and colour would shake a group of plants out of the commonplace. Borders should have an air of rapture and spontaneity, lifting things into the poetic. Russell Page's description of visiting Norah Lindsay's garden at Sutton Courtenay is an inspiration. 'There was a dusty lovely Elizabethan timbered house and a wide walled garden which I remember as a turbulent sea of flowers. One moved along paths through a waist-high haze of pinks and greys … *Salvia turkestanica* with its rough foliage and nacreous bracts, beige, mauve and greyed-pink, used in masses as quiet foil for pink mallows and sidalceas and high old roses, bushes whose arched sprays were heavy with silvery pink blossoms.'

Plants need room. Most people make beds too small, especially a bed under a wall which is dry and maybe shaded part of the day. Borders cannot be too big. They may need paths inside them, although that gets a bit complicated. Borders act as an element which gives mass and colour against the planes of a lawn or the vertical line of a hedge or wall. They need 'body', a repetitive theme of planting. We use euphorbias in this way. Both of us used to feel that they were somehow alien, a feeling which is almost entirely subjective and inexplicable – but in the form of *Euphorbia characias* subsp. *wulfenii*, we both now love and use them endlessly. (Neither of us can yet, nor probably ever will, stomach the burnt-looking *E. griffithii* 'Fireglow'.) Ferns are something we cannot live without and they are so easy to live with – no trouble with slugs with a fern or any other pest or predator much. Pteridology is the thing. We used them in the stumpery we made at Highgrove, and then met Martin Rickard, the world expert pteridologist and fernophile. He was very kind and loved the stumpery and the opportunity it provided for all sorts of ferns to thrive and be popularised. Think of a black and white photograph of ferns of any sort and you can see the beauty in monochrome.

Scented perennial stocks are a constant, a serial monogamy in garden after garden. Yesterday I went back to a garden we had planted six years ago and tried to do a mental audit of what had been pushed out. *Matthiola incana* is always one of the first things to leave. Technically a long-lived biennial or short-lived perennial, you think you have it for life but each year some rot off over winter and after five years you could have none, bar the seedlings in the gravel path that might just have got away with it, or better still been rescued and nurtured. Here, we have alternated stocks with small nameless lavender plants from B&Q, which were bound to be slower growers. The stocks muscled in quickly filling the space between, gaining ground in the first year and filling the air with a divine warmth which used to reach its zenith at Pentecost. The following winter halved their host, and we spent a dispiriting spring pulling out and hacking back the worst affected, but this has given the lavender a chance to really bush out. This spring those lavenders have put on a flush of growth with an underwater lushness that smelled oily and astringent in the rain, mingled with the clove baked into the stocks. This year the matthiola froths through the successful passages of lavender. The *unsuccessful* passages, mutters Mr B darkly, are the bits where my nasturtiums got away and smothered everything. It is true. And Isabel so loved the nasturtiums that she let them lie all dewy and jewel-coloured all over the little lavender plants which faded away. We have three generations of lavender, the lockdown, last year's 'Vera' and this year's 'Grosso', none of which are quite the same. This will mess up the seamless whole, an irritation some gardeners would cope with quite badly. There are a lot of bald patches at the far end of the double avenue, a key element in the garden. Those naughty nasturtiums and the matthiola were only intended as a sideshow while the aromatic hedge got going, and they have distorted the plan. But it is always a tricky balance, the combination was really pleasing this year; from now on it will be something else.

That is the thing with gardens. You need an adaptable turn of mind. Things come and things go. The audit yesterday was a list of those powerful plants which had overcome the others in a few seasons' battling. A list of where to go with the flow, who to execute or try to hold back, and a sad little list of the disappeared. Because it has been so long, all the detail has blurred from the planting. It looks lush and great and, in some places, has taken its own or its owner's course to great effect. We like this, we rate it success. But the list – matthiola, astrantia, eremurus, lupin – all need room to be made again for them, and replacements grown. There we have a plan, but you cannot expect that this will be slavishly adhered to. Nor would it produce the same effect that Mr B's original specific placing of each 9-centimetre pot produced two years later. It's a different thing every year, and in our own garden our fidelity will wander, new friends will be given house room and the thing will be constantly evolving with each season, good and bad results driving the story. It is the dignity of the house, our quiet mistress, that makes this garden. It is grass and trees, hedges and stone, and water that last just a little bit longer.

Epilogue
The Smell of Childhood

The most romantic gardens are born of endeavour. Take the pared-down beauty of Derek Jarman's Dungeness garden: it is about something 'elsewhere', timeless, to do with effort and I think maybe to do with his facing up to death and our complete transience. Romantic places can be solitary, on the edges of wild abandonment – Llanthony Priory, perhaps, under the Black Mountains – or have great refinement, leading the mind to drift like a leaf, as at Studley Royal water garden. Our favourites would appear to be artist's gardens, such as the private delights and obsessions of Monet and Cedric Morris, or the agoraphobic energy of Ian Hamilton Finlay. William Kent was an artist; even the gentleman garden makers, such as Henry Hoare at Stourhead or Charles Hamilton at Painshill Park near Cobham, were artists. Painshill was romantically choked with brambles when I was a teenager and crawled through a forbidden fence on a ring road to get into it. So too Bomarzo in Italy, created in the sixteenth century by a grieving widower, the Count Orsini, to honour his dead wife, Giulia; a *Sacro Bosco*, fantastical and bizarre. Forgotten for centuries, it was still almost unknown and never better than in 1970, when Julian Bannerman climbed in through the thickets, and it unfolded its story before him. The romance of walled gardens, flourishing and abandoned, plucks the heart-strings of most of us. Take the enduring devotion inspired by Frances Hodgson Burnett's *The Secret Garden*. Tim Smit's genius – when caught up in just such a love affair with the gardens at Heligan – was to call them 'Lost'. Rescue is part of any romance, human and gardening. I don't think a romantic garden can be 'designed'. What makes you breathless in a garden, or a cathedral, is the humanity that went into it, the passion, the tender care, the reason and the unhinged quality – that belief that it could work. As Mirabel Osler puts it: 'At the heart of gardening there may need to be a belief in the miraculous.' Beauty must be there and, to my mind, husbandry, which is certainly about ownership on one level, but about responsibilities on another. Husbandry is about tenderness and care; that is what is touching. Have you seen those small high-hedged-against-the-sea back gardens on Iona, productive and lavished with seaweed? Real and romantic gardens are not an act of conspicuous consumption; they are about a different kind of exaltedness, about triumph in the face of adversity, about wit and love. Romantic love is fundamentally about wanting to make a patch with someone, the desire to look after each other and nurture something, to make flowers and fruit, and maybe babies, together and generously. So too, the best gardens are about giving and loving.

Showing off: after an entire childhood of being admonished about it, 'showing off' was what Mr B and I went on to make a career of. Our older siblings remain both enabling and cautionary, especially mine and especially about doing it in print. Mr B is a bit Tommy Brock and good bit Toad of Toad Hall. He loves the open road, is a compulsive doer, and is very lucky in that. It is a blessing to be a self-starter; it gets him up in the morning and off he generally goes, despite his shot knees and other limbs, emptying the rubbish, watering the polytunnel, planning the day. He almost always gets straight down to watering or mowing when we get back from a long journey if it is still light. Clearly, he likes to sit down with a fag and a drink as well, but his modus is 'beachmaster'; he would have made a terrific military man, inspiring loyalty and devotion. Perhaps only the second time he met my mother we went to her antique shop. It was a small eighteenth-century building right next to the giant Christopher Wray Lighting Emporium that stretched along the King's Road; this had a very large clock hanging out over the pavement and was all the address she would give shippers – she would just say: 'Look out for the clock at Christopher Wray's Lighting Emporium. I'm there.' I took my first boyfriend, Mr B, to see her. As in *Lovejoy*, the yellow Volvo estate was parked a bit down the street, lights winking, boot gaping like a hungry chick. Immediately she sweetly commanded Mr B to drag up a large fridge from the basement and take it to the car. Like Obelix he humped it on to his back and walked off smiling. She was impressed. Mrs E, as my brother called her, took some impressing. Propelled as she was by acute impatience, particularly when driving, if an obstacle blocked her way, she would step out of the car waving her driving licence up by her face and say, 'Special Branch: now move along.'

Mr B's mother, Hilda, was as strong but patient, kind and dignified as a duchess. She always told him he would wear himself out and regret a life of labour. She was of course right, but also wrong because the life of labour has kept him remarkably healthy and his soul cheery. This is important for both of us. As we spend the gloaming grooming, gathering-in and watering, it is not just the green bounty and the birdsong which is uplifting, but, subliminally, our mood is altered by the smell of green things, edible, arboreal and floral. On winter nights I try to remember these special qualities of smell and light of summer nights. As I write, it is high summer, and the very bricks and mortar are warmed through like storage heaters. But the longest day always comes too suddenly. Now it is past, the garden under rain has begun to smell musty but comfortable. The briar rose leaf still broadcasts cidery fumes, and moss-rose flowers are gone but their sticky sepals still emit an aromatic smell of books and white spirit. Fig trees, which are anciently understood and without parallel, have those round-fingered leaves of such grace, and the smell of the whole plant radiates its own sun and earthiness. Our sensations are in holiday trim, and the tall hollyhocks wander the Norfolk coast, while broad sunflowers are caked in gold. I have sat for long mesmeric periods in early July watching hoverflies grazing on the anthers of sugared regal lilies, all of us drugged by the scent. Lily perfume is the greatest night incense, even in the pristine virginal madonna lilies and the native martagon lilies. The smell of these is cooler, closer to melon rind than their Asiatic cousins. Then there are night-scented stocks whose smell is white chocolate, reminding me of ballet shoes. Like stocks, all the phlox family smell of brushed cotton. Tobacco plants in the night along with angel's trumpets, now called brugmansia, smell powdery and powerfully narcotic. Angel's trumpets work well in pots. I think that in the evening air their smell becomes more diluted and decorous, when crickets sing and an August moon picks out their pagoda bells, pearly against the dark; most are fragrant in the evenings to attract pollinating moths. *Brugmansia suaveolens* in shades of white, yellow or pink is the most potent and flowers long into autumn. The scent has the potency of lilies but the lightness of *Magnolia grandiflora*, which has perhaps the most magnificent of all summer night scents. In Morocco brugmansias grow as big as pear trees, but they are tender in this country, so you need to take cuttings or just keep them frost free over winter.

This midsummer's night, we had been working on the design of this book with Dunstan all day, and Mr B was determined to stay up and enjoy the shortest night. A night that happened to be perfectly still. A lesson as to how simple garden lighting is the best, he placed a candle in the earth of the pot of a big-trumpeted brugmansia. The silhouette embroidered the house with a William Morris imprint of hanging bells, trembling with magnification. The air vibrated with their scent added to the roses, philadelphus, the muscat-grape smell of the elderflowers and sweet peas mingled with linden, geraniums and jasmine, smells that shield against low feelings. It reminded me of summer nights in childhood fending off sleep.

The man with the child in his eyes, Mr B, has always maintained a strong connection with his inner child, sometimes the toddler. He remembers so vividly his carefree youth, the spontaneity, the lust and the coursing lifeblood. A lightning rod connects him to the ground, the earth coming up through his feet. I found I could not write a diary in 2020; I could not record it, I had childlike feelings of anxiety. It was a childlike sensation that you had no idea what would happen next, very alarming, making one feel very small and inconsequential. Historical Child found me crying in my bedroom, probably after an angry outburst with Mr B, and sweetly reminded me that times were strange. It was all very uneasy but there was a well-spring of content. Normally, we get hoodwinked into thinking we are indispensable in our roles in the outside world, but lockdown showed me that being 'stuck at home' could be made the best of. I know Mr B is not a little resentful that I am prepared to get up at 5.30 a.m. to write a book, but not to prick out and pot on, even in the comfort of the poly-folly – let alone get bone-frozen hoeing or mending hoses. Nothing worse than a wet job on a freezing day. I probably have done my ten thousand hours of that sort of work though – I have the worn joints to prove it; but I have a long row to hoe to pass or fail at the word processor.

* * *

The fact that ours is always an experimental garden is a relief and a bit of a cop out – there is no pressure for it to be perfectly tabulated. We are happy with it patchy and unformed; the haphazard is made into an advantage and there is no moment where it would be best to photograph. There never really is anyway. We are constantly 'picturing' the place; beyond the bones, it is a painting that never dries, dabbed at and daubed, smeared, and scraped off to start again. Much more like the way music is reinterpreted in every playing, every year in the garden is a new performance. Making music or painting is hard work; you might rather be doing something more obviously relaxing, but it is never a chore and you know it might make you feel better. Mr B and I, like a lot of people, love nesting. Violet and I spent happy hours during our enforced time together nesting, making napkins out of bits of material in drawers, and nurturing the hens – our favourite, named Nora Ephron, and her mates – we bought in a flush of panic-buying in the last open days of that Covid March. Violet and her husbandman, Historical Child, listened to my stories and histories and lessons of growing and gardening, off and on, in the day, while Historical Child read Mr B's father's memoirs aloud to us some nights through tearful giggles. Historical insisted on growing delphiniums from seed – they're flowering now – and did digging and delving when his back was okay between online teacher-training sessions. Terrible handicap to be long-backed and Scottish-skinned if you want to be a peasant. Much better the Irish build and rosy complexion of Mr B and Logical Child, who are square and well planted. They both have unparalleled focus. Logical, being a scientist and happiest in the lab with lasers, observed the red admirals sucking on rotten fallen pears in late summer and drew up chairs so that we could sit and watch the floor quietly tipping with the wings of gorging butterflies. Perhaps they had all come from the empty chrysalids which encrusted the inside seams of the Kingswood Scout tent we have up every summer. Logical Child will continue to midwife the solar array with me, and the pizza oven. Emotional Child escaped London later, arrived a little shaken, ripped off his shirt and began work on his Italian skin colour and strengthening his fragile body and soul, making both more wiry with hard work. Heaving things around in the reclamation yard, he showed me how myriad newts, frogs and toads had moved in, lifting the plywood boards to reveal muddy chambers where, darkly earth-coloured and soupy green, their hibernating bodies were posed and exquisite as a fossil tablet.

Then it was summertime in the shrunken lockdown world. A time to clear the endemic weeds and familiarise ourselves with the shadows and soil warmth of different beds. The time was not wasted. The unusual abundance of onions and potatoes, pigeon-torn lettuces and cabbages amazed us all. This landscape of vegetable rows looked like pictures of wartime borders turned over to food production. We could plant carrots, beans and onions as sacrificial planting in any garden we are making. As an opening scene it would help to open up the soil, fix nitrogen, and work down with deep roots to improve any soil.

Lockdown was like a game of musical chairs, the music stopped, and some were chairless, cheerless, isolated. The very lucky, with the chairs, took stock at least. Brought roundly to a realisation of how the back yard, the garden, the great outdoors, the earth is ours to husband.

The J. Parker's catalogue thumped on the mat yesterday, messenger for the call to arms next year. 'Onward' was the motto of Mr B's mother. Hermes the messenger calls us to order bulbs for next spring; to trade, to trust to luck, fertility, sleep, and husbandry.

Follow the developing story at
bannermandesign.com/husbandry

Index

Note: Page numbers in *italics* refer to colour plates.

Acknowledgements

Thanks are owing to all the characters mentioned in the text. With some flippancy. I hope you are not offended because it was not intended, and do please forgive any factual errors and transgressions into fiction. Special thanks to those who kindly, patiently read, corrected and designed with talent and sagacity. Thanks to my sons for all their support and wisdom. And, of course, thanks to the husbandman.

Picture credits
All photographs copyright © Isabel Bannerman, with the exception of the following.

The plans of Ashington Manor Farm on the endpapers were drawn by Helen Phillips, to whom my eternal thanks.

The engraving on page 7 was made in 1819 and published in *Gentleman's Magazine* in 1820.

The black and white photographs of Ashington Manor Farm in the mid-twentieth century, which appear on pages 17, 43, 54, 67, 77, 92, 99 and 117 were given into my hands by someone who had no idea where they came from.